D1447461

Child Custody and Visitation Disputes
in Sweden and the United States

Child Custody and Visitation Disputes in Sweden and the United States

A Study of Love, Justice, and Knowledge

Diane M. Pranzo

LEXINGTON BOOKS
Lanham • Boulder • New York • Toronto • Plymouth, UK

Published by Lexington Books
A wholly owned subsidiary of The Rowman & Littlefield Publishing Group, Inc.
4501 Forbes Boulevard, Suite 200, Lanham, Maryland 20706
www.rowman.com

10 Thornbury Road, Plymouth PL6 7PP, United Kingdom

Copyright © 2013 by Lexington Books

All rights reserved. No part of this book may be reproduced in any form or by any
electronic or mechanical means, including information storage and retrieval systems,
without written permission from the publisher, except by a reviewer who may quote
passages in a review.

British Library Cataloguing in Publication Information Available

Library of Congress Cataloging-in-Publication Data

Pranzo, Diane M.
Child custody and visitation disputes in Sweden and the United States : a study of love, justice, and
knowledge / Diane M. Pranzo.
pages cm
Includes bibliographical references and index.
ISBN 978-0-7391-7134-9 (cloth : alk. paper) -- ISBN 978-0-7391-7135-6 (electronic)
1. Custody of children--United States. 2. Visitation rights (Domestic relations)--United States. 3.
Custody of children--Sweden. 4. Visitation rights (Domestic relations)--Sweden. I. Title.
K707.P73 2013
346.48501'73--dc23
2012048018

♾™ The paper used in this publication meets the minimum requirements of American
National Standard for Information Sciences Permanence of Paper for Printed Library
Materials, ANSI/NISO Z39.48-1992.

Printed in the United States of America

Contents

Acknowledgments

A very heartfelt thanks to all the state court personnel in Connecticut and Florida and court personnel in Sweden who took the time and trouble to answer my requests for information. Thank you for the thoughtful comments and advice from Dr. Pamela Cox, Dr. Lynne Pettinger, and Kate Stanley at the University of Essex, Professor Allison James at Sheffield University, Professor Annika Rejmer at Lund University, and the students at Tsing Hua University, Taiwan. This book would have never been completed if it were not for help from the late Professor Ian Craib who was a "friend in need." A special thank you to my wonderful and very patient family: Erik, Saga, Beata, Yrsa, and Rima.

ONE

Introduction

BEST INTEREST OF THE CHILD STANDARD

In legal cases where parents cannot resolve their dispute regarding how to work out issues of residence, visitation, and custody, the best interest of the child standard is a holder into which will go various definitions by the actors who become involved in the contested case. To add to the complexity of finding what is any one child's best interest, the actors (parents, children, social workers, psychiatrists, psychologists, legal professionals and judges) do not begin their claims of what the definition of best interest should be from similar standpoints. There are three unique starting points for the interpretation of the events of contested cases and so there are competing versions regarding what should be placed inside the holder. Love, justice and knowledge as concepts representing these actors can aid in comparing the way in which the people involved in custody and visitation cases begin their interpretation of both the events of and other actors in a case. Out of each of the three spheres come competing claims regarding the correct information or background needed to define what is in the best interest of a child who is the subject of a case. The legitimacy of the claims made by each sphere and the role those claims should play in defining best interest are not equal among the three spheres and only justice has the ability to make claims of truth or fact.

In both Sweden and the US, the best interest standard underlies decisions made in reference to children where there is a dispute between parents concerning their children. Sweden and the US have signed agreements affirming that they will respect custody decisions made in each other's jurisdictions.[1] The fact that the best interest standard is used by both societies is the legal basis for respecting the decision-making process

1

of the other. A comparison of the two societies that focuses on the interaction between the interpretations of the events of a case by the actors, through their lenses of love, justice or knowledge, brings out features of decision making that would be unavailable to a researcher studying only one society. Do parents, for example, in both Sweden and the US make basically the same claims? Can they, and do they, use the same frames of reference when they give their evidence? What cultural features impact on their descriptions to the professionals and to the court? How do professionals and experts describe the parents, children and events in a case? What cultural proscriptions frame the understanding of the experts and professionals? How do these taken-for-granted understandings impact on decision making and outcomes for children? How do the judges filter the evidence they are given in order to define best interest? What cultural features might impact on judges' interpretations and what they define as best interest? This book attempts to give a clearer idea of what the answers to these questions might be.

CHILDREN'S BEST INTEREST AND SOCIALIZATION THEORY

The best interest of the child standard is a modern and ethical improvement in decision making in cases where decisions are being made that will impact on the life of a child. In the past, children were considered property of their fathers or other male guardians and were obliged to accept the interests of those persons over their own (Mason 1994; Singer 2000). Currently, in decisions made about children the court has to consider what is best for the children subject to the decision regardless of the wishes of their parents. At the same time, definitions of what children's interests are have been affected for the past half century by the idea of proper socialization of children based on functionalist theories. The idea of socialization has profoundly influenced our understanding of children and what needs should be ascribed to them. Functionalist theories of society outline the way in which children take in and adapt to their society. In this conception of "the child," a child is viewed as separate from society and as being continuously socialized mainly through the influence of the family. If all goes well, eventually the child becomes a well-functioning member of society. In functionalist theory, the fundamental necessity for the formulation of a theory of socialization is not concerned with children as such, but rather is an attempt to theorize how adults come to take their place in a properly functioning system (Corsaro 1997, 10). Also, and crucially, children are viewed as being a possible threat to the functioning of the system (to society) until they are successfully socialized (Corsaro 1997, 10). Although functionalist theories have been found to be limited in the ability to explain the operation of society in general, the underlying assumptions in much social science research and literature pertaining to children, as well as our modern common-sense understanding of children's needs, have been and still are significantly influenced by ideas regarding the socialization needed to maintain a properly functioning system of society. The idea of correct socialization of children impacts on the definition of best interests, because the interests of children come to be viewed as what is good for children as future well-functioning members of society (and it is this definition which often impacts on law and policy), rendering definitions of children's interests set in the moment subordinate to that definition.

SWEDISH AND US SOCIETY COMPARED

In *Three Worlds of Welfare Capitalism,* Gøsta Esping-Andersen (1989, 26-29) compares US and Swedish society. According to Esping-Andersen, modern capitalist societies can be grouped by the ideal type of welfare regime with which each society is most closely identified. These regime types say something about the societies which lean most closely to instituting them. According to Epsing-Andersen's typology, Sweden can be categorized as a *social democratic welfare regime* and the US as a *liberal welfare regime*. The social democratic regime type points to a focus in Swedish society on particular ideals. One of these key ideals is the drive to institute equality in society. This focus on equality is driven by the understanding of relations between people, as well as how such a society deals with conflict. As Swedish ethnologist Åke Daun (2004, 105) points out, equality for Swedes is conceptualized as sameness; that is, people are conceptualized as being no different, no better, and no worse than any other member of society. Because each person is the same and deserves a similar outcome in life, it should be the duty of the state to try and further equality of outcomes for people in society. The idea of equality as sameness (*jämlikhet*), of society-wide security (*trygghet*), of cooperation (*samarbete*), of just right moderation (*lagom*), and of togetherness (*gemenskap*) are concepts that form the secular moral and ethical underpinning of Swedish society and that contribute to the Swedish understanding of conflict. Social welfare concentrates on the relationships between people and on the responsibilities that people have toward one another in the areas outlined above. These responsibilities are given legitimacy by a society-wide commitment to promoting care and equality through the use of state institutions and social welfare provisions. One of the features that characterizes the Swedish social welfare regime is the stature and importance of the institutionalized idea of care. *Care* is defined and provided by the state through the idea of a society-wide "cradle to grave" safety net. The elevation of care as a duty of the state is beneficial to members of Swedish society, yet it can also carry with it a subtle repressive and paternalistic quality; state institutions define the discourse of care through the knowledge and work of state professionals (social workers, teachers, etc).

In a liberal welfare regime such as that in the US, equality is the idea of separate individuals united by rights in common. In this sense individuals are responsible for their own life situation as well as the outcomes attributed to their private choices. Equality is often discussed in the US in terms of equality of opportunity. But, in a sense, since each individual is conceptualized as being responsible for making his or her own opportunities, equality in the US still returns to the idea of individuals linked by a conception of rights in common. In the US people are not viewed as being the same and the state is not viewed as responsible for helping to provide similar outcomes for its citizens. Instead, everyone is conceived of as possessing the same set of rights with which they can proceed to interact equally with other individuals (citizens) of US society.

These two regime types tell us something about the expectations of people toward the role of the state and its institutions in the US and Sweden, and the regime types tell us something about the focus each society takes regarding the interaction between people. The members of US and Swedish society turn toward different state institutions and have widely differing expectations of the state. In Sweden, people are turned toward the institutions that dispense social welfare provisions. A member of Swedish society can expect a certain level of state social support. They expect care from teachers, doctors, social workers and mental health professionals when they require such care. On the other hand, in the US, people focus on a conception of themselves as members of a society with certain entitlements derived from what they conceptualize as their rights as citizens. In this sense they are oriented toward viewing law as the domain in which those rights can be confirmed or enforced. Certain members of US society may make use of social services provided by the state; however, social services are regarded by the US population as something to avoid contact with. In the US people do not happily, or readily, seek out the care provided by state professionals unless they are compelled to do so. Although most US citizen do not promote their rights on an everyday basis, US society can be viewed as turned toward legal institutions of the state as the place where their rights as citizens can be enforced. The phenomenon of "the legal" can be seen in the way in which US society is permeated by depictions of "the legal" which points to the focus on law and its institutions. Depictions of rights in action are ubiquitous in US society, in fictional films and TV dramas that include courtroom scenes as well as in the popularity of "real life" Court TV, and in the everyday use of phrases such as "I know my rights" and "demand your rights" that have a distinct currency in the US which does not resonate in Sweden. The comparison can be put this way: Sweden is a community of relationships between people who are viewed as the same, whereas the US is a community of right-bearing citizens. Swedish citizens have expectations toward the state for care. US citizens have expectations toward the state to enforce their rights.

The discussion of the differences between the two societies as exemplified by Esping-Andersen's typologies is more than simply an overview of the two countries in this study. These models provide a starting point for understanding the differences in how events of a case might be framed by the actors in the cases and how best interest will be defined, because differing perceptions of conflict arise from the way in which relationships between people are viewed in each society. These differences in ideas regarding conflict can be brought out through a brief discussion of the role of metaphors used to frame conflict.

CONFLICT BETWEEN INDIVIDUALS OR CONFLICT AS MISUNDERSTANDING

Understanding conflict in terms of the metaphors around which different conception of conflict are framed helps to visualize the impact ways of viewing conflict will have on court processes in the two societies (see, for example, Lakoff and Johnson 2003). Conflict can be understood as romance following White's (1973, 191-263) archetypal themes.[2] When conflict is understood through the lens of romance, conflict is perceived to be an event that takes place between individuals who are engaged in a struggle or quest. The resolution of conflict involves the individual in the conflict proving he or she is right. In this sense, at the end of a conflict there will be an individual who is viewed as right and an individual in the wrong. The individual in the wrong is characterized as the cause of the conflict. In this view of conflict, however, refusal to compromise can also be seen as proof of the rightness of one's position and tenaciousness in the face of adversity. A conflict viewed within the frame of conflict as romance focuses the cause of conflict on individuals. Although doggedness in the face of all the odds is to be valued in the party who is in the right, this same stance is not valued in the party perceived to be the cause of the conflict. At the root of conflict is seen to be an individual whose refusal to admit that he or she is not in the right keeps the conflict from being resolved. In court the refusal of the individual who is wrong to see that they are incorrect implies an *unreasonable* person.

Alternatively, conflict can be viewed as comic as when people lack information or misunderstand a situation. In such a situation lack of understanding can lead to hilarious events (for example, mistakenly getting into the wrong bed in a hotel, because it is dark and all the rooms are so similar). Conflict is viewed through a lens of comedy in the sense that people take inappropriate actions or say inappropriate things because they lack the whole picture; they misunderstand the situation. The conflict as comedy metaphor frames conflict as an event that happens in the relationship between people. People are not wrong or right; they just lack information. It is the lack of information within the relationship between people from which a conflict arises. If conflict is viewed as a misunderstanding there is no right party and no wrong party; there is merely a misunderstanding that needs to be uncovered which reasonable people will then work to correct through compromise. The framing of conflict as comedy or conflict as romance impacts on the discourses of justice and knowledge. The two ways of viewing conflict orient the definition of the problem of lack of agreement between the two parents and so identify where the source of the conflict will be viewed as arising from and how the events and actions of participants in the cases will be explained. Individuals in either society have the possibility of viewing events from one or both of these starting points, however the US can be characterized as a society which tends to view conflict through the *conflict as romance* metaphor and Sweden as a society which tends to view conflict through the *conflict as comedy* metaphor. In the US the focus is on the actions of individuals. The individuals may view themselves as the person who is the hero of the case (that is, the person who is right). It is just as likely, however, that the concentration on individuals in a conflict leads to the search for and the framing of individuals as the cause of the problem; that is, the definition of the problem of lack of agreement regarding questions of custody, residence or visitation can be found in some aspect of the personality or character of the individuals in a case.

In Sweden the concentration is on relationships between people. Conflict happens in relationships when the people in those relationships misunderstand events or each other's meaning and intentions. In this situation the definition of the problem is not to be found in identifying the individual responsible, but in trying to identify the misunderstanding that exists in the relationship between the people involved in the conflict. The metaphors of conflict in the two societies provide a frame for the stories that are constructed regarding the events of a case. It provides the starting point where problems of nonagreement are to be found.

COMPARING DOCUMENTARY EVIDENCE

One of the most interesting features of the court documents used in this study is also the feature which makes the texts difficult to analyze; namely, the authority of the narrative contained in the documents once it has been put down in writing. Breaking outside the narrative which the actors have created is difficult, because the written word and a coherent narrative both lend credibility to the version of events given in the documents. This is especially true when the story is written by someone carrying a particular kind of authority such as a judge. It is therefore the job of the researcher to try to unravel the representations of the participants (especially parents and sometimes children) which, like characters in a book, are drawn to construct particular people. Although the researcher cannot replace her own version of events with those given in the text, she can show how events in a text came to have a particular narrative version and can demonstrate that alternative versions may have come into being if the evidence had been framed differently. As Fairclough, (2003, 40) has pointed out, "order making devises within a text lend themselves to the promotion of the legitimacy of the story contained within it." The narrative character of the court processes in the documents produced by these processes are not surprising. We are constantly making sense of events in the world through the process of trying to logically order events and ascribe a coherent meaning to those events. Narratives are the process by which people make sense of all that is "out of the ordinary" or "whatever does not conform to everyday expectations"; that is, whatever events require "explanation," according to Bruner (1990, 47). The idea of sense making is a key component of comparing what is happening in the processes in the US and Sweden, because narratives formed under such conditions of sense making have a cultural specificity. Different societies consider different situations to be out of the ordinary or not, and have different ways of arranging and framing what is considered out of the ordinary.

ASSUMPTIONS IN THE TEXTS

A researcher can also show which assumptions were in operation during the construction of court narratives. What is said in a text is often based on a background of what is assumed but not explicitly written (Fairclough 2003, 40). Identifying the unsaid assumptions of a text helps in the comparison of the texts between the two societies, but also helps us to understand the conclusions that will be drawn from the story of the events as developed by a judge or report writer. Some assumptions that are current in both the US and Sweden are hinted at in the documents but not always explicitly. The following four assumptions are the most prevalent of these: 1) Claims of violence are often or mostly tactical; 2) Child sexual abuse allegations in disputed custody cases are most likely false and most likely a tactic used to gain custody; 3) Trouble in the father-child relationship is a problem often or mostly instigated by mothers; 4) Parents who insist on sole custody are uncooperative. Throughout this study I both explicitly and implicitly engage with these assumptions; that is to say, it is sometimes questioned whether an actor depends upon one to frame the story they have created, or whether or not the evidence from this study lends support to the reality of the assumptions or seems rather to be drawing conclusions that put the validity of these assumptions in doubt.

WHO REPRESENTS THE CHILDREN?

In both Sweden and the US, the child's voice is often (when they are not giving the opinion directly to the court) mediated through a professional or expert, or a professional or expert is required to assess if the child has anything to say which, in the opinion of the professional or expert, should impact on the decision. In the US sample cases, children were represented by a guardian ad litem (GAL). Additionally, in the Connecticut sample there were custody evaluators known as family relations counselors who carried out the custody evaluation. In twenty cases there was an attorney for the minor child (the AMC, who represents older children in Connecticut). All these professionals had the opportunity to draw conclusions concerning what represented the best interest of the child and to listen to what children were saying. However, all these professionals and experts could draw different conclusions and offer differing recommendations to the court. In a few sample cases (US27, US34, US35, US36) the GAL was the only professional making a recommendation to the court.[3] The role of the guardian ad litem in US custody cases has been criticized for the lack of a clearly defined function regarding their role and the varying levels of credentials needed in order to practice (Johnson-Weider 2003, 77; Ducote 2002). The US report writers were much more apt to paraphrase what the children said than were the Swedish evaluators. The physical aspects of the interview, for example, where the interview took place in the US cases and other references to context were not commented on although the custody evaluation carried out by the family relations counselors had lists of the meetings that were conducted specifying whether the meetings were "home visits" or "office visits."

In the Swedish cases, the social report writer's role was not exclusively to interact, interview, and advocate for the child in the case. Usually two social workers were working together to write the custody evaluation. They were likely to be the only professionals making recommendations in a case and only one recommendation was produced from their combined effort (this was usually the case, although there was one sample case where they disagreed, SW40). The work was not divided into the one who spoke to the parents and the one who spoke with the child. In other words, the social worker who interviewed the child in the Swedish cases was also the professional writing the custody evaluation. The Swedish social workers were the only professionals who interviewed the child and presented a recommendation to the court. The Swedish reports almost always contained descriptions of the home environments of the two parents and interaction between the parents and child. It was standard, in the Swedish custody evaluation, to contain a short interview with the child's nursery school or school teachers. Additionally, without asking the children outright where they wanted to live, the Swedish report writers tried to see if children had any opinions regarding the situation even when quite young children were the subject of a case. In order to arrange opportunities for children to voice an opinion the report writers used techniques meant to engage the children in a conversation rather than just asking a series of questions. They might, for example, use dolls or drawings of the child's family. Since some interviews in the Swedish sample appeared to be verbatim accounts of what children said, it was less apparent where the voice of the professional intervened (what had been paraphrased) or additionally, what the professional chose to put in or leave out.

In the US cases the voice of the child was most often mediated through the professional or expert. There could be more than one professional collecting information in order to make a recommendation to the court. The professionals and experts involved in the cases, the GAL (or attorney for the child in the case of older children in the US), the social worker and the psychologist, can be thought of as starting their collection of evidence from three different perspectives based on their professions. Each of these perspectives impacted on what significance the professionals and experts attributed to a child's opinion. The different ways of viewing the evidence of a case could both color what evidence the professionals and experts presented, or impact on what opinions of the child the expert or professional left unsaid. The GAL and particularly the AMC might view their role as a legal advocate for the child's wishes (the GAL is often a lawyer): someone whose role involves reporting what the child's wishes are and advocating for those wishes. In the Connecticut cases, there was some indication that GALs viewed being an advocate for the child's voice as their role in the process. In case US30, for example, the GAL recommended residential custody to the father, because the children expressed the desire to move back to their old neighborhood even though the father was violent toward the mother and maliciously disruptive of the children's education. The perception of their role as advocate for a child's opinion, however, was not the uniform view of GALs even in Connecticut. In some jurisdictions, such as the Florida jurisdiction in which the sample cases were collected, the GALs carried out the same function as the family relations counselors did in Connecticut. In this case, the GAL seemed to act as less of a legal advocate for children's wishes and instead took on a role closer to that of a social worker. Social workers such as the family relations counselors in Connecticut who carried out custody evaluations, looked at many factors, such as the suitability of the parents as custodians. They also tended to view the children's opinions as one more piece of evidence that might have greater or lesser significance in deciding the case depending on how they viewed the other evidence they collected. Psychologists, in the US cases, had the task of evaluating both the parents and the children in the cases where the court ordered psychological evaluations. Discovering the child's opinion for the psychologist did not involve finding out what a child wanted for the sake of having the child express such an opinion (as in the Swedish cases), but as part of the psychologist's analysis of the thought processes of the child. A psychological expert in a case may view the recitation of the child's wishes as merely the mistaken statement of the child's confused emotional state.

LIMITS OF THE STUDY

The two societies looked at in this study, Sweden and the US, share the most similar characteristics in legal processes that use the best interest of the child standard to decide issues of custody, residence, and visitation where a dispute between a mother and a father is involved. The laws governing processes that involve parents and nonparents or same-sex parents are less similar between the two societies and even between US states. The best interest standard is also used in child protection cases, but such cases are beyond the scope of this study.

The majority of cases included in the study were collected from Connecticut with the help of two clerks of the court and two law librarians. Court documents were selected under the criteria of cases involving two parents disputing issues of custody, residence, or visitation. Responses from jurisdictions in Florida resulted in the collection of case documents from those jurisdictions with the same criteria as above. The cases continued to be collected until similar themes could be consistently identified across the material with each new supplement of documents. The limitation of this method is that the researcher has to depend on the voluntary contribution of the person answering the inquiries made. This limitation is in part linked to the confidential nature of some of the documents in the cases.

The US material includes cases with highly detailed information. Some cases, for example, contain the custody evaluation reports (the documents of the court social worker or GAL) and the court minutes, the latter of which provides a transcript of what was said at the trial. Other documents included are the court summary and the court document referred to as the *memorandum*. These documents contain the summing up and give the judge's reasons for the orders made. Included in the analysis of the US cases are appeals court decisions which are used to balance the impressions arising from the anonymous and coded US court documents, especially in reference to those cases that were very detailed. The appeals court decisions were included in the analysis in order to identify which detailed features of the anonymous cases could be generalized relative to events happening in the decision-making process across the US. Scott (1990, 20-35) advocates the use of a range of documentary materials to add support to arguments made on the basis of single sources of documentary evidence. Despite variations across state jurisdictions in the US, it is possible to posit that the underlying social and cultural features outlined in this study that are exhibited in the Connecticut and Florida documents exist across the US. Although there are differences between state laws, individual US states look to each other to find solutions for problems which all state courts face in deciding contested custody and visitation cases. The *Uniform Child Custody Jurisdiction and Enforcement Act* (1997), for example, was written so that law in this area would be compatible throughout the 50 states to discourage forum shopping by requiring every state to respect the decisions made by courts in other states.[4]

The cases that are identified with an anonymous ordering system come from the Regional Family Trial Docket in Connecticut and two Domestic Relations Divisions of counties in Central Florida. They are labeled US1-US67. These cases are taken from court records between the years 1996 and 2005. The locations within Connecticut and Florida are not given where the excerpts of the cases appear in the text for reasons of anonymity for the participants linked to those documents. In the case of the US the term *trial court* is used in this study to refer to the lowest court. Different jurisdictions refer to this court of first instance by various titles, as shown above in the case of Connecticut and Florida. Trial court refers to the court where all the evidence will be heard and all testimonies will be made, the case will be decided, and an order made. In contrast, the appeals courts only review trial court decisions, and do not hear new evidence. The additional material used to analyze the US cases includes appeals court cases between the years 1996 and 2005. These additional cases come from Florida and Connecticut and other jurisdictions within the US. In total, 238 additional cases have been analyzed to support the conclusions drawn from the anonymous US sample. Appeals court cases and trial court documents sometimes use the names of participants and many are reported in official published reports. In these cases, when an excerpt is taken from one of these documents, the full citation is given.

The documents for the Swedish study refer to court documents from the Swedish *tingsrätt* (trial court) which has the same responsibilities as outlined above for the trial court in the US. Different courts in Sweden were contacted using the same criteria outlined above for the US documents. Fifty-three court processes are used as the basis of the Swedish comparison. These documents are numbered SW1-SW53 and are taken from the period between 1996 and 2005 from 21 different Swedish tingsrätt. When excerpts are used from the Swedish cases the specific tingsrätt the case is taken from is not stated for reasons of anonymity. A deliberate attempt has been made to avoid the possibility that someone might recognize themselves or be recognized. Additionally, all the excerpts from the Swedish documents have been translated into English by the author. The Swedish documents contained custody evaluations and the trial court's summing up and the order made but no verbatim minutes from the trials. Additional materials, for the Swedish cases, include government documents from the *Statistika Centralbyån* (Statistics Sweden) and the Swedish *Rikstag* (Parliament).[5] More information on the methods used in this study, as well as detailed information about the case material, is provided in the appendix.

THE TERMS USED IN THE BOOK

The terms *residence, joint custody, sole custody, visitation* and *contact* are used in this book. *Residence* is the term used to define where the child will live. Custody, as it is awarded by all the courts in the sample cases, is meant to be exercised by both parents (except in the case of sole custody) even when the child does not live with both parents. Residential custody refers to parents who have the child/children living with them the majority of the time on a regular basis. The term *visitation*, as used in this study, is interchangeable with the word contact and refers to an arrangement of meeting times between a parent and a child when they do not live together.[6] *Parenting time* refers to the time a child spends with a parent whether or not the parent is the resident parent. In both the Swedish and the US case excerpts, the words *mother, father,* and *child* have been substituted for real names or the legal titles used in the documents. This book also makes a distinction between experts and professionals that is sometimes blurred by the self-conception of these actors' own roles. *Professionals* is the term used to refer to individuals with particular skills gained through training and practice in that skill, specifically social workers and lawyers.[7] *Experts* is the term used to refer to individuals who have gained a particular specialized knowledge (especially of psychology) through learning. Expert opinions are given legitimacy through the expert's link with fields of knowledge which include scientific methods and extensive training in those methods, especially testing. Experts include clinical and forensic psychologists and psychiatrists. Professionals include custody evaluators and guardians ad litem.

THE STRUCTURE OF THE BOOK

The chapters in the book are organized around a comparison of the cases in relation to the three types of actors in the cases and the sphere of knowledge claims they represent; that is, justice, knowledge and love. Before turning to the analysis of the case material, however, chapter 2 takes a brief look at the historical changes in decision making which have resulted in the current use of the standard, best interest of the child, in the US and Sweden. Chapter 2 also considers the impact that the differing legal traditions in the US and Sweden have on the process, especially in reference to the use of discretion in the decision-making process. The structure of the contested process and a review of the legal criteria which directs decision making in both Sweden and the US is reviewed. Finally, differences in the ideal of mother role versus father role are viewed in terms of the impact such ideals have on the definition of continuity. Chapter 3 then turns to analyze the role of justice through a comparison of the US and Swedish material in cases where transfers of residence and/ or custody are being considered. Chapter 4 compares the role of knowledge in the US and Swedish cases by analyzing the techniques used by the professionals and experts as they develop their recommendations in the cases. Chapter 5 looks at the interaction between the aspects of justice and knowledge discussed in chapter 3 and 4. The construction of events and representation of the actors in the cases as interpreted by the court, professionals, and experts are illustrated in a close analysis of three cases where there are problems with visitation. Chapter 6 focuses on the role of love and the resulting claims parents make regarding their parental roles and what those roles should mean in terms of the definition of best interest of the child. Contested areas involving the issue of care for the children who are the subjects of the processes are examined. Chapter 7 looks at parental narratives concerning violence and the impact that accusations of violence have in the conflict over arrangements for custody and visitation. Children are at the center of the conflict, but what role do their opinions and wishes play in the process? Chapter 8 analyzes and compares the differences between the two countries in terms of the underlying basis for including children's opinions and the impact that these different starting points have on the reception of children's opinions in the decision-making process. Chapter 9 examines the role that the interaction between love, justice and knowledge played in the process in the US and Sweden and discusses the conclusions that can be drawn from the study.

NOTES

1. Hague Convention on the Civil Aspects of International Child Abduction (25 October, 1980).

2. White specified the archetypal themes of human existence found in literature as romance, comedy and tragedy.

3. In Florida, cases US27, US34, and US35. In these cases, as well as the Connecticut cases, where there was a GAL, the GAL was a lawyer.

4. Uniform Child Custody Jurisdiction and Enforcement Act (1997), signed into law in 49 US states.

5. Statistika Centralbyån, www.scb.se and the Swedish Rikstag (Parliament) www.riksdagen.se/ www.regeringen.se/ also, Svensk författningssamling (SFS) www.riksdagen.se/webbnav/index.aspx?nid=3910.

6. However, there could exist cases where parents are allowed contact through cards and letters but not necessarily physical visitation. Nevertheless, this was not an issue in any of the sample cases.

7. When discussing professionals, either social workers or lawyers, I am referring to the people making recommendations to the court regarding children and not lawyers representing parents.

TWO

Laws, Process, Parental Roles, and Continuity

This chapter briefly reviews the history of decision making regarding the custody and care of children in both the US and Sweden and the development of the best interest of the child standard. The legal traditions found in the US as compared with Sweden are considered along with a review of the areas of similarities in custody criteria and the process which governs decision making in custody and visitation cases. Differences are found between the two processes in the application of discretion, and finally, differences are evident in the gendered ideas of parental roles in US society as compared with Swedish society. The implication of these differences on the interpretation of continuity is discussed.

CHILD CUSTODY DECISIONS IN HISTORY

The historical features of child custody decisions in the US have been recounted by Mason (1994), who traces the changing legal basis of decisions regarding children along with the social and political context of those changes up to and including the best interest of the child standard. During the colonial period in the US, legitimate fathers held rights over their children that were almost absolute. Changes occurred slowly during the period Mason terms "the New Republic." Small changes moved child decisions in the US toward a more sentimental concentration on an ideal of maternal love (49-83). Children began to be viewed as people with interests separate from the interests of their fathers. The ascendancy of the idea of maternal love needed by young children resulted in decision making according to the *tender years* doctrine in which very young children were viewed as needing the specific kind of gendered care mothers provided.[1] Slowly during the middle of the last century, the science of society utilized by social workers started to play a key role in decision making. The increasing frequency of divorce, along with the relaxing of divorce law, led to an increase in the number of parents going to court to have custody questions settled by a judge.[2] In the early and mid-twentieth century the tender years doctrine removed the need to define the best interest of the child standard more clearly, but by the late twentieth century US courts began to reject the idea that mothers were almost always the most suitable parent to care for children. Gender-neutral decision making, which promoted the idea that both parents had the capacity to provide nurturing care for their children, was written into most statutes in the United States by the middle of the 1970s. Soon it became impossible to base a custody decision solely on the gender of one of the parents.[3] As mothers lost their legal status as the default custodial parent, the concentration on keeping both parents involved in the life of their children came to be viewed as one of the most important factors in disputed child decisions. Ideas regarding joint custody and shared parenting became popular. The idea of the *best interest* of the child, which earlier directed only child protection decisions, had eclipsed first the absolute right of legitimate fathers over their children, and later the preference for mother custody. By the late twentieth century in the US, the standard no longer had any firm principles for defining it.

Singer (2000) provides the historical background to changing perceptions of childhood and parenthood that have impacted on child decisions in Sweden. According to Singer, the idea of best interest of the child has had a long history in Swedish law,[4] although the content of what was thought of as being in a child's interest has changed dramatically according to the period in which decisions were made (87). During the earliest period Singer reviews, children of divorced or unmarried mothers remained in the care of their mothers until age three, at which children were given into the care of their fathers, who would be responsible for their children's care until children were about seven years old, at which time both parents became responsible for their children's care. If the father was unknown the child would remain in the care of the mother (Sjösten 1998, 21). During the eighteenth century, fathers were considered the guardian of their children whether or not they married the child's mother. If a married mother's husband died she became the legal guardian of her children when she turned twenty-five. Unmarried mothers were under the control of their own guardians and never became guardians of their own children, although they might have the actual responsibility for their children's care (1998, 21). Singer describes how already at the turn of the nineteenth century, the plight of children of unmarried mothers led to stricter laws governing the declaration of a presumed father for children who were born of unwed mothers (2000, 60). At this time, there was an effort made by the state to have fathers take responsibility and provide for the children they had fathered outside of marriage. At this time unwed mothers became both custodians and guardians of their children born outside of marriage. If unwed parents agreed, the father could obtain guardianship as well, or the court could order guardianship to the father if the mother was unfit. In the latter half of the twentieth century, the increase in divorce led to discussion regarding the consequences of divorce for children; at the same time, contested custody conflicts became more common (Rejmer 2003, 17). In Sweden, as in the US, the idea of gender neutrality in custody decisions between parents emerged in the middle of the twentieth century. The law was changed to allow fathers to obtain custody of their children born out of wedlock without having to prove the mother unfit.

In both countries, the move away from the preeminence of father's rights and later the gender-neutral forum of the custody process, which ended the use of the tender years doctrine, left court decisions in custody cases with less predictable outcomes. A range of factors to be considered by the judge developed in Sweden and the US. In the US, contested cases started to depend on professionals and experts with social work or psychology backgrounds who specialized in interpreting the needs of children and the actions and claims of parents.[5]

LEGAL TRADITION, CUSTODY CRITERIA, AND PROCESS

Sweden has a Roman civil law system, similar to many parts of Europe. The Swedish system of law looks to codified laws in order to render decisions. In contrast, most of the US depends on a common law tradition which looks to case law or precedent.[6] Nevertheless, although the legal traditions of Sweden and the US differ, there are more points of similarity than differences in contested cases both in the core values encapsulated by law in the area of child decisions, and in the contours of the structure of contested custody and visitation processes. The three jurisdictions, for example, which are the main focus of this book, Florida, Connecticut, and Sweden, all clarify that decision making should be made according to the *best interests of the child*. Florida statutes make clear, for example, that "The court shall determine all matters relating to custody of each minor child of the parties in accordance with the best interests of the child."[7] Similarly, Connecticut statutes provide that, "In making or modifying any order as provided in subsection (a) of this section, the rights and responsibilities of both parents shall be considered and the court shall enter orders accordingly that serve the best interests of the child."[8] Swedish statutes makes clear, "The child's best interests shall be placed first in all decisions made, according to this paragraph in all questions of custody, residence and contact."[9] Separate statutes govern disputed custody processes in the fifty US states; however, overlap occurs in the criteria governing disputed custody decisions (Elrod and Spector 2010, 972-973). Sweden and all fifty US states have laws specifying that decision making should be carried out on a gender-neutral basis.[10] Florida, calls for "An equal assessment of fathers and mothers in determining a child's residence."[11] Swedish law states, "No parent, on the grounds of their gender, is more suitable as a custodian for the child than the other parent."[12] Linked with the gender-neutral forum of the court, there is a strong value in Connecticut, Florida, and Swedish law placed on children having a relationship with both parents. Florida makes this point clear, stating:

> It is the public policy of this state to assure that each minor child has frequent and continuing contact with both parents after the parents separate or the marriage of the parties is dissolved and to encourage parents to share the rights and responsibilities, and joys, of childrearing.[13]

Swedish law echoes this value, "Decisions regarding what is best for the child should be made with special regard to . . . the child's need of near and good contact with both parents."[14] Connecticut emphasizes the continuing responsibility parents have to maintain the other parent in their child's life, specifying that the judge consider this feature in decision making:

> The willingness and ability of each parent to facilitate and encourage such continuing parent-child relationship between the child and the other parent as is appropriate, including compliance with any court orders.[15]

In Florida, the statutory list twice underlines the "most friendly or cooperative parent" principle by stressing the weight given to the choices of the parent most willing to facilitate the relationship with the other parent.[16]

The importance of continuity for children is a key value. For example, Florida law specifies "The length of time the child has lived in a stable, satisfactory environment and the desirability of maintaining continuity," as well as "The permanence, as a family unit, of the existing or proposed custodial home." Similarly, Connecticut specifies "The length of time that the child has lived in a stable and satisfactory environment and the desirability of maintaining continuity in such environment."[17] The wishes and preferences of a child who is the subject of a decision may also be given weight in most US jurisdictions. In Connecticut, for example, "Any relevant and material information obtained from the child, including the informed preferences of the child," can be considered and weighed with the evidence of a case.[18] In Sweden, the law governing contested custody states that the child's opinions should be considered.[19] The value placed on considering children's opinions in the Swedish process is followed up in the law that governs the social services and the work of social workers conducting custody evaluations.[20] Domestic violence and child abuse can be a factor in all three jurisdictions.[21] In Florida, making a false allegation of abuse can also be a factor.[22] Many US states, especially Connecticut, depend heavily on case law to guide decision making; the factors to be considered in defining the best interest standard are found in the criteria represented in precedent. Since 2005 in Connecticut, the criteria for decision making has become codified to a greater extent than in the past; however, the current statutes are made up of criteria which judges had previously sourced from case law and were already utilizing.[23] Recently, Sweden has moved away from a presumption of joint custody to allow for less prescriptive decision making in cases where one parent is asking for sole custody.[24] Florida retains a presumption of joint custody, but can order sole custody if it is in the best interest of the child. Connecticut has a presumption of joint custody where parents have agreed to it; however, where one parent does not agree a judge can order conciliation, and can order sole custody for one of the parents if the judge finds sole custody is in the best interest of the child.[25]

SIMILARITIES IN THE STRUCTURE OF THE PROCESS

In both countries, despite differing legal traditions, decision making in contested cases includes features of both the adversarial process and the inquisitorial system. The custody dispute process is adversarial in that the parties to the dispute are involved in making a *good case;* that is, the parents or their lawyers are compiling and presenting evidence in a way that supports the demands they are making for a particular order.[26] The process also contains elements of the inquisitorial system, because in contrast to a typical adversarial process, in which the judge acts as a type of referee, in contested custody and visitation cases the judge is also the trier of fact.[27]

In both the US and Sweden, the process is confined to the type of issues that the court can make a decision on. The legal parameters of a case must be decided on before the trial, as the following statement exemplifies, "The court is precluded from entering a judgment on any matter outside the issues framed by the pleadings."[28] In both the US and Sweden, the preliminary stage of the process involves a pretrial meeting. In this meeting the specific areas on which the court can rule are marked out and explained to the parents in order to follow the mandate given above. There is a possibility for the parents to come to an agreement at certain points during the early part of the process. Early on in the Swedish process, for example, the head judge tries to help the participants come to an agreement. If this does not help the couple they attend cooperation talks (*samarbetessamtal*) with a social worker. If none of these avenues leads to an agreement, then a custody evaluation is carried out by social workers from the Department of Social Services. The evaluation usually involves home visits and observations of each parent's interaction with the child or children. It might involve more than one such visit. After the custody report is finished and read by the parents, the parents can decide to come to an agreement instead of going on to trial. If no agreement is reached a trial is held. Swedish custody cases are heard not by a single judge, but by a panel of four judges (Saldeen 2002, 471-510). The panel includes one judge trained in law (*lagfaren domare*) and three lay judges (*nämndeman*).[29] Coming to a decision involves a discussion of the evidence by these four individuals. The final judgment in the Swedish cases almost always contains a unified voice of the court. The Swedish professionals writing the custody evaluation work for the Department of Social Services which is separate from the judicial system, but is nonetheless a state agency and governed by laws regarding children which are in agreement with the laws and values followed by the court.[30]

The basic outline of the process in Connecticut and Florida is similar to the Swedish process in that there are pretrial meetings and early attempts at mediation (however, parents can choose to hire private mediators).[31] In Connecticut mediation takes place with a social worker who is employee of the court system (family relations counselor). The family relations counselor has a similar position to his Swedish counterpart. The parents in the Connecticut cases are ordered to attend parent education classes.[32] If an agreement is not reached by the parents as a result of the pretrial mediation then a family relations counselor is assigned to carry out a custody evaluation. In these evaluations there is on average one home visit to each parent's home when the child is present, and sometimes an office visit together with each parent and the child/children. Each parent is interviewed together with the child/children at least once when possible. Expert evaluations, when ordered by the court, include psychological testing and evaluations and take place at the clinical facilities of the expert. One noteworthy difference between the US and Swedish process is the number of professionals and expert witnesses (in addition to the family relations counselor) who are involved in US cases. In the majority of the US sample cases there was a guardian ad litem (GAL) who also made a recommendation to the court. In the Florida sample cases the custody evaluations were carried out by the GAL. In the majority of the 47 US cases where there was a GAL present; the GAL was a lawyer by profession. The GAL was a special representative of the child in both the Connecticut and Florida cases that did have a counterpart in any of the Swedish cases reviewed in this study. In both Connecticut and Florida, when expert assistance was determined to be necessary, expert testimony was given (for the most part) by a person with a Ph.D. in psychology (a few cases involved a psychiatrist).[33] The US cases were more likely than the Swedish cases to include experts hired by one or the other of the parents. These experts were usually in private practice or worked for a clinic not under the control of the court or social services.

DISCRETION IN FAMILY LAW CASES

Discretion is a key feature in both US and Swedish contested custody cases. Discretion refers to the freedom available to the judge to make decisions on a case by case basis in which each case may involve a different weighting of similar criteria, allowing for more fluid decision making given the context of each specific case; however, the use of discretion is stronger in the US. Discretion can be seen, as Dillman (2002, 165-185) puts it, "as a way for competing values which are incorporated in the law to be decided on a case by case basis." The vagueness of the standard, best interest of the child, necessitates, and is meant to allow for, the weighing of values that conflict. It also allows for unspecific factors to guide decision making on a case by case basis; however, from discretion arises the possibility that the personal beliefs and bias of judges will be incorporated in court decisions. Philips (1998, 48-87), for example, depicted the way in which judges in Arizona apply their political beliefs to such seemingly fail-safe structures against discretion as plea bargaining. Investigating the role of judicial discretion in contested divorce cases in New York, Garrison (1996, 505-27) concluded that judges could sometimes be shown to follow statutory mandate. Other judicial decisions, however, showed that discretion allowed for following the privately held values of individual judges.[34] Crucially, Moran points out that extensive discretion can impact on parents' perception of fairness despite the fact that it is the freedom of US judge to choose from among various sources of evidence and decide what weight these factors will be given, which is meant to instill rigor and legitimacy in the process in the first place (2003, 361).

US judges can justify their strong use of discretion in any given case due to the multiple places they have to source and legitimate their decisions. For example, the inclusion of many professionals and experts, all with competing versions of the evidence and conclusions to be drawn from the evidence, allows US judges to construct new versions or implications from the evidence presented by the experts and professionals. In the sample cases, the strong use of discretion by the US judges, in comparison with the Swedish courts, leads to less uniformity in the outcome of US decision making. Swedish cases, for example, most often conclude with the court following the conclusions of the custody evaluation. This state of affairs explains why, although the Family Law Code in Sweden is not as detailed as are statutes in many US states regarding the specifics of custody criteria, this lack of specificity does not lead to greater discretion for the Swedish court.

Kelman (1981, 221-237) illustrates another difference between US and Swedish law that impacts of discretion. In a comparative study of Swedish and US occupational safety law, Kelman found that the intention lawmakers have when they write a law directs decision making in Swedish courtrooms.[35] In contrast, in the US a political issue may result in a law being written, but judicial discretion when applying the law may accord more or less weight than was actually intended during the process leading up to the passage of a law. In contrast, *högsta domstolen* (high court) rulings in Sweden correct lower court decisions which are not applying law in the way it was intended when it was written, through ruling on a particular case that illustrates the general rule for lower courts.[36] Unlike in the US, the Swedish court does not use multiple sources from which to pick and choose pieces of information in order to build a definition of best interest. Instead, the Swedish panel of judges tends to identify the correct definition of best interest from the competing claims given in a case. For example, the custody evaluators present one definition of best interest in the form of the completed custody report. Each parent puts forward their own definition of best interest. The panel of judges most often views the custody evaluator's definition as the correct definition if the evaluation is in accordance with the strength and meaning of the relevant laws. The social report writer (custody evaluator) was the only professional submitting a report to the court regarding custody, and the only professionals (there were usually two custody evaluators working together) to interview both parents and the child or children. The Swedish panel of judges either agrees with the assessment of the professional, or determines that the professional does not understand the strength of the value implied by the law, or that the social worker does not understand the law which needed to be applied and so offered a recommendation which was not in accordance with law.[37] The Swedish court disagreed with the social report in only three cases.[38] At the same time, this fact should not be taken to mean that Swedish courts merely rubber stamp the recommendations of social workers. Rather this state of affairs demonstrates that there is a fit between the weight given to particular values provided for in the rules and laws that guide the social workers carrying out the custody evaluation investigation and the law the judges are applying.

Discretion in the US custody process, on the other hand, allows US judges to construct a definition of best interest. For instance, a US judge may agree with the GAL's schedule of visitation, but agree with another professional or expert who is giving evidence regarding who should have residence.[39] The judge may even reference her own sources of knowledge or experience which have led to the decisions she makes. Nevertheless, US judges must make good arguments for their decisions, and cannot simply disregard statute or case law, nor can they make decisions which appear to have no basis in the facts of a case without the possibility of a parent appealing the decision.

PARENTS AS EQUAL AND DIFFERENT OR EQUAL AND THE SAME

As seen in the beginning of this chapter, the history of custody decisions in both the US and Sweden is a history of the changing rights and roles of parents toward their children. The idealized role of parents, along with the impact of gender on these perceived roles, differs between the two societies. There are some areas of similarity, however, for example when parents with children separate in the US and Sweden they most often choose the mother as the resident parent (Arendell 1988, 19; Kurz 1995, 152-153; Mnookin and Maccoby 1992; Mnookin and Maccoby 2002, 54-88; *Barnen och jämlikheten*, 2000). In Sweden about 80 percent of single parents are mothers, and in mixed families (that is, step-relationship families) more Swedish mothers (than Swedish fathers) have children from their previous relationships. 20 percent of Swedish children whose parent do not live together, however, live in joint-residence arrangements (Statistiska centralbyrån 2004, 13).

Despite the similar gendered way in which the majority of noncontesting separating couples solve issues of where children will live, the ideals of gendered parent-child relationships in the US and Sweden are different in ways which impact on contested custody decisions. In particular, a discussion of the differences in the perceived roles of mother and father in the US compared with Sweden is necessary for understanding the operation of the criterion of "continuity" and the criterion of "having a relationship with both parents" as key influencing criteria for decision making by judges in both the US and Sweden. Differing ideas found in the value of the ideal roles of mothers and fathers as parents impact on the idea of gender equality and gender neutrality. In the US, the gender equality of parents is viewed as the equal value of two inherently different parent figures. Viewed as different but equally important, fathers and mothers both have indispensable roles to play in the development of their children. A popular book on fatherhood, for example, sums up the US ideal of a distinct difference between father care and mother care in the following quote:

> Thus begins my tale about how fathers do not mother . . . it takes work to fully comprehend how it is that men can become nurturing beings and how fathering differentiates itself from mothering. Herein lies a central question for this book: if fathering differs from mothering in fundamental ways, are there things that only a father can give their children? (Pruett 2001, 18)

In this version of fatherhood, no one but a child's father can fulfill the father's role which will assist children in being properly socialized into society. Mothers, on the other hand, are viewed as the parent with a unique role linked with a particular nurturing gendered image of maternal care with a linked psychological impact on a child's development and future psyche. At the same time as these gendered views of parental roles are present in US society explicit gendered parental roles need to be shed when US parents enter into a court process where these gendered roles are replaced by gender-neutral terms and criteria which act as a cipher for the previously gender-laden images of care. Primary caregiver becomes a veil for recognizing the gendered type of care mothers usually carry out (without attributing such care specifically to mothers) and the criterion of "having a relationship with both parents" signals the value given to promoting or maintaining the relationship between fathers and their children. The more gendered construction of parental roles in the US impacts on the understanding of conflict, which in turn has consequences for the definition of what will be determined to be in the best interest of a child, particularly in those cases where there is a conflict between a primary caregiver mother and the perception of the loss of the father-child relationship, as will be shown in subsequent chapters. In contrast, in Sweden, the ideal is that the role of father and mother is the same; part of the duty of the state through its welfare regime is to ensure the ideal of gender equality as sameness through provisions such as state-sponsored and -run daycare which has made it possible for most mothers to return to work while their children are still young, and through the promotion of generous parental leave for fathers allowing fathers to spend more time in the day-to-day care of young children.[40] The relationship between fathers and children and mothers and children is not viewed as crucial through a particular reference to a gendered parental role, but instead the ideal is that parents are crucial as parents to their children. Mother and father as "the same" in Sweden may be an ideal, but the ideal drives attitudes, actions, and expectations. Specific parent-child relationships may be viewed as irreplaceable, but not irreplaceable by reference to the gendered role of mother or father which only a mother or father can fulfill. This view of parenthood can impact on decision making and particularly on the consideration of continuity. Continuity becomes linked, to a greater extent in the Swedish context, to keeping children in their familiar environment rather than viewing continuity as consistency in a child's placement with the parent who represents continuity of care. The equal emotional role of both parents to their child, along with the view that care by either parent will be similar regardless of a parent's gender, is assumed in Sweden in cases where there is an ongoing relationship between children and both parents. The criterion of a "relationship with both parents" is linked to a greater extent with the idea as it is encapsulated in the United Nations Declaration of the Rights of the Child (UNCRC); that is, providing children with a continuing relationship to both parents is an obligation of society, and is propelled less by the idea of detriment for children and society due more specifically to the worry regarding the gendered idea of father loss.[41] In cases where a parent-child relationship is estranged, for example, there is less of a drive to create a relationship where none exists due to the idea that fathers or mothers have a unique, specific and irreplaceable gendered role in the lives of children in general.

CONTINUITY

Both US and Swedish courts stress continuity as a key component of the reasoning for regarding a particular decision as being in the best interest of a child, but different definitions of continuity in the US and Sweden change the weight given to the claim made by one parent to be the primary caregiver. In the US sample cases, the term *primary caregiver* has more significance as a support for a judge's decision, and it is the privileging of this criterion that judges had in mind when they designated one of the parents primary caregiver. The role of continuity becomes particularly important to assess in cases where the parent-child relationship with the non-resident parent has become estranged but where a transfer of residence to the estranged parent is being considered. The relationship of primary caregiver and child in the US cases is viewed not only as the physical care of a child, but is linked to the attachment of the child to her psychological parent and the consideration of the impact on the child's psychological development and future mental health if the child's residence is transferred. While discretion clearly allows for decisions to be made that do not award residence of the child to this psychological primary caregiver such decisions seemed to elicit from the US judges (particularly in Connecticut) a need to explain why the judge decided against the strong weight usually applied to continuity of care.[42] In the majority of the US cases, the judges viewed the mother as the parent who represented continuity of care for the children, and many mothers received residential custody of their children if not their desired custody type (44 out of 67).

In contrast with the US cases, the judges and the social report writers in Sweden stressed an idea of continuity focused on environment rather than on care; thus the emphasis was on keeping children in their familiar surroundings rather than, strictly speaking, with a primary caregiver. Swedish legal praxis does specify the importance of considering the attachment of very young children to a primary caregiver (most often their mothers) as being a factor that should be given special weight.[43] However, the brief period of infancy where a differentiation is made between the caring role of mother and father is short and is quickly replaced by the ideal of two parents who are the same in the type of bond and experience of care they have with their children. The judges and custody evaluators in Sweden did not focus on whether a child was accustomed to being cared for more by one parent than the other. Additionally, it was taken for granted that both parents were capable of carrying out proper care; that is, both parents had the ability to see to their child's physical and emotional needs on a daily basis unless case specific factors made it clear this was not the case.

This chapter has shown how the idea of the best interest of the child standard developed from a concentration on fathers' rights to mother love and finally toward the process seen in today's courtrooms. The areas of commonality in the values encapsulated in the laws in both Sweden and the US result in a process which is similar in many respects despite differing legal traditions. Differences start to be apparent, however, in the role and use of discretion, and in the ideals of motherhood and fatherhood which give rise to differing interpretations of continuity and having a relationship with both parents. The next chapter looks more specifically at the comparison of US and Swedish cases especially in reference to the criteria of continuity and of having a relationship with both parents.

NOTES

1. Determining unfitness could include the consideration of a mother's moral fitness.

2. The number of contested cases is around 20 percent in the US; however, the number of US cases that come to full trial is less than 20 percent. The percentage is lower in some US states, such as California, where there is mandatory meditation (Johnston 1994, 165-182). According to Rejmer, in 2000 there were 5938 cases of conflict coming to the court in Sweden, which makes the figure around 10 percent (2003).

3. See, for example: California Family Code Section 3040-3048: "In making an order [a court] shall not prefer a parent as custodian because of that parent's sex." New Jersey Permanent Statutes 9: 2-4 "Custody of child; rights of both parents considered. In any proceeding involving the custody of a minor child, the rights of both parents shall be equal." Missouri Revised Statutes 8.452.375: "As between the parents of a child, no preference may be given to either parent in the awarding of custody because of that parent's age, sex, or financial status, nor because of the age or sex of the child."

4. Singer (2000, 48; especially note 3) provides an example of the *best interest* of the child standard in use in Swedish law from around the seventeenth or eighteenth century. Such references begin later in the US, at about the end of the eighteen century.

5. Goldstein, Freud and Solnit (1984) contributed greatly to the idea of looking to the psychological needs of children in child custody decisions.

6. With the exception of Louisiana, which maintains its civil law tradition.

7. Florida Statutes Title 6 chapter 61.13 (2)(b)1.

8. Connecticut General Statutes Chapter 815J Title 46b-56 (formerly Sec. 46-42).

9. Föräldrabalken 6 kap. "Om vårdnad, boende och umgänge" § 2. a(SFS1949:381) with amendments up to and including SFS 199798:7.

10. See, for example, California Family Code Section 3040-3048: "In making an order [a court] shall not prefer a parent as custodian because of that parent's sex." Or, New Jersey Permanent Statutes 9:2-4. "Custody of child; rights of both parents considered. In any proceeding involving the custody of a minor child, the rights of both parents shall be equal." And also, Missouri Revised Statutes 8.452.375: "As between the parents of a child, no preference may be given to either parent in the awarding of

custody because of that parent's age, sex, or financial status, nor because of the age or sex of the child."

11. Florida statutes Title 6 chapter 61.13 (b)1.
12. NJA 1989 s.335.
13. Florida Statutes Title 6 chapter 61.13 (b)1.
14. Föräldrabalken 6 kap. "Om vårdnad, boende och umgänge."§ 2. (SFS1949:381) with amendments up to and including (SFS 199798:7). See also Högsta Domstolen references: NJA 1986 s. 338, NJA 1989 s. 335 and NJA 1992 s. 666, specifying that the parent most likely to promote a relationship between the child and the other parent is the most suitable as the custodian.
15. Conn. Acts 258 § 3(c) and Conn. Stats. § 46b-56(c) (2006 supp.). Criteria became more codified after a change in the law.
16. Florida Title 6 chapter 61.13 (3) (a). The parent who is more likely to allow the child frequent and continuing contact with the nonresidential parent. (j) The willingness and ability of each parent to facilitate and encourage a close and continuing parent-child relationship between the child and the other parent.
17. Florida Title 6 chapter 61.13 (3) (d). and Conn. Gen. Stats § 46b-56(c) (2011) Statutory factors at 10.
18. Conn. Acts 258 § 3(c) and Conn. Stats. § 46b-56(c) (2006 supp.).
19. Föräldrabalken (SFS1949:381) with amendments up to and including (SFS 199798:7). See especially 6 kapitel: 2a § 2b §3§.
20. Socialtjänstlag [Social Service Law and Regulations].
21. Florida Title 6 chapter 61.13 (3)(l). Evidence of domestic violence or child abuse.
22. Florida Title 6 chapter 61.13 (3)(k). Evidence that any party has knowingly provided false information to the court regarding a domestic violence proceeding pursuant to s.741.30.
23. There are a few areas where judges have powers they did not have previously. For example, the power to make therapy a provision of the judgment.
24. See Regeringens proposition 2005/06:99 and NJA 2007 s. 382.
25. Connecticut Chapter 815j Sec. 46b-56a; Florida Title 6 chapter 61.13 (2).
26. Keeping in mind the differences between an adversarial system and an inquisitorial one, in the inquisitorial system the court is involved in determining in the facts of the case compared with the adversarial model in which the judge acts as an impartial referee. In the contested custody process the US judge steps out of this role and is also the trier of fact. However, in both Sweden and the US the process appears as an adversarial one in the sense that the two opposing sides are trying to make a good argument for the order they are requesting the court to make.
27. In case US12, for example, the court found that the mother's accusations against the father were false. Some states still have the possibility of a jury trial in family cases, Texas, for example, but this was not a feature of any of the sample cases.
28. Corpus Juris Secundum, CJS PARENT § 124: Scope of inquiry.
29. Föräldrabalken, (SFS1949:381) with amendments up to and including (SFS 1997/98:7). Especially 6 kapitel (Om vårdnad, boende och Umgänge) 6:5 § and Föräldrabalken (20:1).
30. Socialtjänstlag [Social Service Law and Regulations].
31. The Florida court from which the cases come did not have mandatory mediation at the time the cases were decided but currently does. See: Rule 12.200. Case Management and Pretrial Conferences: Florida Family Law Rules of Procedure (Continuing Legal Education Publications, The Florida Bar, Tallahassee, Florida, 2004) and Rejmer 2003, 91-113. Also see Connecticut Superior Court, Procedure in Family Case Management Matters, with amendments up to January 1, 2006: Chapter 25 General Provisions, Sec. 25-50, (the Secretary of the State of the State of Connecticut). Currently in Connecticut, pretrial meetings to help disputing couples come to an agreement without a trial are held with special masters (lawyers). Additionally, a judge may meet with a couple prior to a trial to try to help them reach an agreement.

32. Conn. Gen. Stats. §46b-69b. The parent education classes are mandatory at divorce for parents with children and most sample case parents attended but a few did not, such as the father in case US31.

33. Twenty-nine US cases involved a court-appointed psychologist.

34. As she puts it: "The statute books today grant judges almost unlimited discretion in divorce cases."

35. The lawmaking process and the documentation produced from that process is meant to direct the correct application of the law.

36. Hovrätt and Högsta domstolan decisions direct the decision making of the tingsrätt toward the correct way of applying the relevant law (that is, direct it to be applied the way the lawmakers intended), rather than offer a source for legitimacy of the decision, as in the cases in Connecticut or Florida. Recent hovrätt or högsta domstolan (High Court) decisions were not mentioned specifically in any of the sample cases.

37. In Rejmer's study the court agreed with the social report's conclusions in 92 percent of the cases (2003, 129).

38. See Table 3, Case Features and Outcomes in the appendix.

39. US judges agreed with the combined opinions of the professionals and experts in 26 out of the 67 sample cases in which there was a custody evaluation; however, they agreed with the opinion of only one of the professionals (and not the other professional or expert) in 34 cases.

40. Historically, even in Sweden, fathers have been less likely to take advantage of the parent leave available to them. The Swedish state has engaged in various initiatives to increase the uptake of the this social provision by fathers which seems to have made some impact in the last ten years.

41. See, for example, the recognition of the right of a child to information regarding his or her genetic origins in the United Nations Convention on the Rights of the Child, Part 1, Article 8, 1989. Sweden was the first country to make it possible for persons conceived from donor sperm to get information about the donor (Gunning 1998, 98-102).

42. *Azia v. Dilascia*, 780 A.2d 992 (Conn. App. Ct. 2001). Florida statutes concentrate less on psychological parent/attachment figure. Nevertheless, the US concentration on a particular type of psychological knowledge in reference to child development renders the primary caregiver, typically the mother, crucial in the future mental functioning of a child.

43. Svedin (1989, 53) an MD in child psychiatry, advocates that "small babies need the parent they are most attached to, mainly mother." And "older children need the parent of the same gender." See also Ewerlöf and Sverne 1999, 70-73: "Mothers are viewed as more suitable as custodians for infants and girls, and fathers are more suitable for older boys."

THREE

Transferring Residence

This chapter concentrates on cases where a transfer of custody from the residential parent to the nonresident parent was being considered. Judges in the US sample cases gave greater weight to placing children with the parent who represented continuity of care for a child (the primary caregiver) in initial residence placements, while the Swedish court did not. Despite this fact, US judges transferred residential custody more often than did Swedish judges. What is the explanation for this difference?

CHARACTER ASSESSMENT: REASONABLE AND UNREASONABLE OR COOPERATION DIFFICULTY?

In the US cases the focus on individuals as the source of the problem directed the process in a particular way whenever the criterion of having a relationship with both parents was seen to be in jeopardy. This led to the US court creating a story which defined one individual who would have normally represented continuity, the primary caregiver, as the cause of the problem and as clearly not the best choice for residential custodian of the child. In the US sample cases the judges' arguments for their decisions in this respect emphasized the need for strong reasons in overcoming the weight they accorded to continuity of care.[1] In case US19, for example, where the judge transferred residence and custody to the father, the judge stated:

> I normally believe continuity of care should be the touchstone. [The judge in the court minutes.]

Focusing on the identification of one individual as the cause of the problem of lack of agreement, the US judges outlined their stories of unsatisfactory primary caregiver in the cases where the judges decided not to give the primary caregiver residence or custody. The identification of the individual who was the cause of the problem of lack of agreement tied in with one of the most important components in the decisions utilized by both the US courts and Swedish courts, namely the assessment of the character of the parents. The trial portion of a custody case, when the parents come into court to give their testimony, allows the judge to personally assess the parents and to regard their testimonies in the light of this assessment. The assessment of the character of the parents has an impact on a judge's interpretation of any other evidence the judge is given by the parents or information she is given about the parents, especially the evidence given in expert or professional evaluations. This axiom of the judge's role, which is meant to provide legitimacy to a court's decision, is a given in the trial court process. As the judge makes clear in case US8:

> The court has had the opportunity to view the parties first hand and assess the circumstances surrounding the dissolution action, in which such personal factors as the demeanor and attitude of the parties are so significant. [The judge's statement in the court memorandum.]

This distinct feature of the trial court is the reason appeals courts often give as justification for not going against a trial court decision; that is, the appeals court did not see and assess the character of the witnesses firsthand as the trial court did. This feature of the trial court also holds in the case of Swedish courts. However, the focus on misunderstanding in the relationship as the cause of the problem of lack of agreement made explicit character assessments unnecessary in the explanation for judges' decisions and so the Swedish judges did not make character assessments an explicit part of the decisions.

The US concentration on individuals as the source of the problem of lack of agreement led to the greater emphasis on character assessment of the parents in US decisions. The US judges could be critical in their conclusions against both parents, as case US7 makes clear, and both parents could be viewed as "the cause of the problem":

> [S]uffice it to say that the parties' relationship, their mutual care of the child, as well as this trial was marked by manipulation, lying, vindictiveness, hostility, and what can best be described as guerrilla warfare. [The judge's statements in the trial court memorandum.]

In the cases where the US judge made an argument for transferring or awarding residence to the non-primary caregiver, however, the picture presented against the primary caregiver involved an interaction between the stress on individual personalities by the US experts and professionals and the character assessment portion of the process. US judges, for example, use the idea of reason in their character assessments. The character and actions of the actors in the cases were viewed by the judges using a frame of reasonableness or unreasonableness. Similarly, the discourses of knowledge in the US use the concepts of irrational action or thought. The discourses of knowledge and justice which involved interaction between concepts of reason and concepts of irrational action given by the experts and professionals will be analyzed more fully in chapter 4. For the moment it is important to note that it is the connection between the narrative of the US experts, focused on the idea of rational and irrational action of individuals, and the character assessment of the US judges, focused on conceptions of reasonable and unreasonable individuals, that framed the narrative of the court in decisions that went against the primary caregiver retaining residence. In their justification for not leaving a primary caregiver as the resident parent, the US judges developed a story of the primary caregiver parent as not reasonable. In case US13, for example, the mother was described as having a volatile temper (although this did not involve a safety issue in terms of violence toward the child):

> The [mother] has a volatile temper. Often when the [father] would call to confirm a visitation time, a conversation would ensue in which the [mother] would create an argument out of a real or imaginary slight. If she did not get a satisfactory response from the [father], she would shout at him over the phone with the child within earshot, frequently using profanity, and would refuse to allow the child to go on the upcoming visit. [The judge's statement in the trial court memorandum.]

The mother's non-cooperation with father visits was viewed as arising from her own unreasonable character. The father was not described by the court as having played any part in the conflict. All the father's actions were described as reasonable in view of the mother's unreasonable character. Father was, for example, very frustrated by the mother's interference with his visits with the child and with mother's personality generally. He tried to cooperate with her as much as possible, according to the court narrative, yet on one occasion she became so confrontational that the father lost control and tried to choke her. The court accepted that the father was remorseful for this incident and that he was an otherwise reasonable person driven to the limits of his patience over the course of time by the mother's unreasonable behavior. Custody was transferred to the father and the mother was given a schedule of visitation.

As in case US13, if the primary caregiver was viewed as the individual responsible for the conflict the criteria of ensuring having a relationship with both parents came into direct conflict with the strong weight given to continuity of care. Ensuring a relationship with both parents involved the US judge's assessment, among other factors, of the "most friendly parent principle." The most friendly parent principle is a predictive criterion that aims to try and determine which parent will be the most open to the relationship between the children and the parent who becomes the nonresident parent. The most friendly parent criterion can add strength to a judge's decision when she is making a case against the usual weight given to continuity of care in cases where custody is awarded to the non-primary caregiver. This aspect of decision making is prominent in other US jurisdictions in addition to Connecticut. In the case *Giles v. Giles*, for example, the primary caregiver mother was viewed as too angry to promote the relationship between the children and the father:

> Citing appellant's demeanor, language, and the evaluator's report, the district court concluded that appellant had a great deal of anger toward respondent that prevented her from fostering the relationship between respondent and the children.[2]

In *White v. Kimrey*, keeping in mind the strong weight that is given to not changing a previous custody order, the resident parent's anger toward the non-resident parent was viewed as a sufficient change in circumstance warranting a modification trial and ultimately a transfer of residential custody:

> After careful thought, consideration, and review the court has determined that a substantial material change in circumstances has occurred. Mother's ability to provide the more nurturing home for child has been tainted by her constant efforts to thwart the father-daughter relationship. She admitted that she told father that she would drop child support if he would sever his parental ties with child.[3]

In a study comparing custody decisions over a 100-year period, Mason and Quirk (1997) argue that the biggest change in US court custody determinations over the last hundred years in the US is the most friendly parent provision now incorporated into most state statutes or criteria for custody determinations. Other studies support Mason and Quirk's thesis (Borris 1998; Davis 2001; Dore 2005). In the US cases, this factor is often linked with a psychological assessment of what might be termed the *least friendly parent* (as in case US13). The least friendly parent involves the negative psychological assessment of a parent who is viewed as interfering with visitation or is not sufficiently positive toward the child-nonresident parent relationship. The US judges seemed to reason along a line in which there was a direct link between the definition of proper care of children and a resident parent promoting their child's relationship with the other parent and this judgment could involve a reflection on an action that had already taken place, or it could be a prediction of what a parent might do or fail to do in the future. The judge in case US13, for example, claimed that

> Her interference with that relationship has had adverse consequences for her child's development. Her failure to have the empathy and the self-discipline necessary to foster that relationship bodes ill for her ability to help [child] meet his other developmental milestones. [The judge's statement in the trial memorandum.]

Clearly the judge in case US13 viewed the resident parent's inability to promote the child's relationship with father as symptomatic of her inadequate care more generally and as evidence of her inadequate care for the child in the future. There was no analysis made by the US judges of whether or not securing a relationship between the child and the nonresident parent by transferring custody would disrupt the residential parent's relationship with the child; that is, whether securing a relationship between the child and the current nonresident parent might be to the detriment of the current resident parent's relationship with the child in that the parents merely reversed roles, but problems with visitation still persisted. In case US19, for example, after a transfer of residence due to mother's lack of cooperation, the father did not follow the court's admonishment to cooperate with the mother. Case US19 is described in greater detail in chapter 5. In case US31 the father disappeared for two years with the two children after residence was transferred to him.

In contrast, the Swedish judges produced a picture that was not overtly judgmental of the individual character of the parents. The language of the judges in the Swedish sample cases was subtle and not pointedly critical toward either parent. The language used in the Swedish cases was seldom more critical of one parent than the other. Specific judgments regarding one parent's bad behavior were noted by referring to other legal proceedings; for example, if a parent had been accused and found guilty of abuse, of threatening, or of violence against the other parent. More often than not, the narratives of the Swedish judges summed up with a focus on what was described as the cooperation difficulty (*samarbete svårigheter*) between the parents. The Swedish judges focused on what they perceived as the problems in the couple's relationship. The court text stressed in its conclusions what both parents could do to change the situation, as in case SW53, where there was trouble in the visiting relationship between the child and the nonresident parent. In the excerpt below, the Swedish judge urges the father to try and gain the mother's confidence and trust by attending to some of her concerns even if they seemed trivial to him:

> In order for the parties to work together what is needed is for [father] to see to it that [mother] can build up her confidence in him. . . . If [mother] decides that [child] should not eat [a certain sweet] then [father] needs to, in order to build up [mother's] confidence in him, to respect [mother's] wishes and not in order to make a point take a stand that will lessen [her] trust in him as a co-partner. Without the parents' actions being characterized by flexibility and attentiveness for the other parent's wishes a working cooperation cannot come to pass. In that case, the ones who will suffer will be the children. [The court's statement in the custody order.]

The Swedish court text was often more inquisitive, as if trying to deduce a solution to a mystery of where the lack of agreement could be found. The following quote illustrates this point:

> Behind the struggle for custody it is not clear whether there is some mutual personal conflict between the pair. [The court's statement in the custody order.] Case SW4

The parents were often firmly, yet without negative comments being made about them as individuals, directed to remember that it was the interest of the child that was at stake. This is demonstrated in the following excerpt:

> The custody question here has not so much to do with how the parents act toward each other, and such things that were touched on in this case. This custody battle is a classic example of parents' intention to hurt each other and attack each other in their child's name. The court in this case, cannot escape being pushed into the partner's argument. Their presentations have developed to the point that they [focus] on their own worth, the whole time forgetting the point of the child's best interest. [The court's statement in the summing up.] Case SW5[4]

In addition to the rarity of occasions in which the court singled out one parent for chastisement, the Swedish court never suggested a course of therapeutic action, nor did it suggest a need for such action. Admitting to one's problems and seeking help for those problems, however, as in the case of alcohol abuse, could make the difference between obtaining joint custody or not, as in case SW9 where the mother admitted to her alcohol abuse problem. Such behavior helped to support the idea of the Swedish court that even a parent with a difficult problem can be cooperative (and reasonable) and so joint custody should not be ruled out by such a factor alone.

The Swedish courts also put a high value on the idea that it is in the child's *best interests* to have a good and close relationship with both parents.[5] This value, however, was given the most weight in cases where placing the child with either parent would ensure continuity of environment, particularly if the custody conflict was taking place at the same time as the breakup of the parents. In this situation either parent might be described by the social report writer as representing continuity of care, and a designation of primary caregiver was not so apparent or important in reaching a conclusion. Consequently, the parent who seemed to be the most likely to cooperate with the children's relationship with the other parent (the most friendly parent principle) had more weight added to their case. In case SW1, for example, father's cooperation with visitation when he had one of the children in his care was not good, but mother's cooperation was determined to be adequate:

There has not been any evidence that she has in any instance been
against or worked against contact between the children and [father]
during the time she has been sole custodian. According to his testimony [father] has during this time had extensive contact with the children.
[The court's statement in the summing up.]

Just as in the US case sample, however, there were times when the value
of ensuring that a child had a relationship with both parents was at odds
with the weight given to maintaining a child in the familiar environment.
In the Swedish court's description the conflict was framed around the
understanding that the problem was a problem of relationships or a misunderstanding between the parents. This view did not result in the use of
problems with visiting as a window on the personality of the resident
parents or the primary caregiver. In the Swedish court's view the problem was to be found in the interaction between the couple. Since the
cause of the conflict was viewed as arising mutually between the parents,
problems in the relationship between the nonresident parent and the
children did not become a sign of the detrimental care of the primary
caregiver. Additionally, the guarantee of securing a relationship between
children and their nonresident parent, which could be ensured by removing children from their familiar environment, was viewed as unnecessary. There was an assumption, in the Swedish cases, that the parents
were reasonable people embroiled in a misunderstanding, but who
would follow the court order once it was made. Given this assumption of
the parents as normal and reasonable people, to remove children from
their secure and familiar environment and caregiver was a severe over-
reaction, even in very contentious cases such as SW16, where problems
with visitation were difficult and ongoing. In case SW16 there was trouble getting the children to cooperate with visits to see their father; the
children refused to go on their scheduled visits. Despite the ongoing
trouble, the court did not want to disrupt the children's lives by transferring custody to the father, which would have involved changing the
children's familiar environment in order to ensure the father-child relationship. Additionally, although mother was not considered blameless,
as the excerpt below shows, the court did not view the situation as evidence of the mother's impaired mental processes or emotional state.
There was no censure of the mother's character and the court did not link
mother's ability more generally to provide the children with proper care
to her inability to get the children to follow court orders. Instead the court
concluded that there was a mixture of reasons why the situation had got
to the point it had. In the view of the Swedish court, the mother was
definitely not acting as an effective partner parent:

[W]hat has come out of the times when [father] visited [mother] at
home to pick up the children or visit with them there, is that the idea
that [mother] actively worked against visitation is not strictly speaking

accurate. At the same time, [mother] is not always helpful to the visitation taking place. It is apparent from the social report that she, already
from the beginning did not like the weekday visitation that had been
decided, that visitation could not be carried out without constant tele-
phone contact between her and the children. This instead of handing
over the responsibility to [father] and trying to motivate the children to
accept contact. [Court's statement][6]

In case SW4, the mother had been the primary caregiver when the child
was an infant. However, during the current custody trial the father had
residence with the child for the preceding three-year period. Although
the mother claimed father was not cooperating with her schedule of visits
with the child, the court did not view the trouble of visitation as a prod-
uct of the father's interference. Instead, the court cleared up the mystery
to the misunderstanding. The problem was not, in the court's view, in
one parent's actions or personality but in the distance between the parents' homes:

It has not been evident from the case that [father] has sabotaged [moth-
er's] contact with the daughter. The answer here lies in some other
reason, for instance; [father's] work schedule; and [mother's] lack of
funds which means she does not have the money to travel to [place] in
order to have the contact she is entitled to. [The court's statement in the
summing up.]

Once the mystery is solved in view of the logic of conflict as misunderstanding the result should be parents who act cooperatively, thus allevi-
ating the need for any future involvement by the law. There was less
emphasis put on the *potential* of the residential parent to thwart visitation
than was found in the US cases. Instead there was more taking for
granted that parents would carry out visitation according to the court
order.

ALLEGATIONS OF CHILD SEXUAL ABUSE

The topic of allegations of child sexual abuse is relevant in the context of
understanding what features incline US judges to put aside the weight
given to continuity of care and the status of primary caregiver and to
transfer custody to the nonresident parent or award custody to the non-
primary caregiver. These cases also encompass similar features to US
cases where there are problems with the nonresident parent's relationship with his/her children and visitation; in cases where there were allegations of child sexual abuse there were most likely to be problems with
visitation. This can be explained by the fact that when an allegation of
sexual abuse of a child was made, in the sample, it was most often made
against the nonresident parent. This was the case in all the US sample
cases where such allegations were made.[7] This fact sets up a situation

where the allegations could be viewed as interference in the parent-child relationship. In all the modification cases where such an allegation was made, the allegation and the problems with visitation were what led the accused parent to ask for a transfer of custody. As in cases with more general problems with visitation, child sexual abuse allegations by one parent against the other parent impacted on the assessment of the accusing parent's character in the US cases.

In case US31, for example, the mother's allegations against the children's father were viewed as symptomatic of problems with the mother's personality and so impacted on the court's assessment of her care of the children:

> I don't think that anybody has asserted that she is not a concerned parent, not a loving parent, not a parent who does not apprehend the needs of her children in some way, but she has consistently refused to acknowledge that she has shortcomings which interfere with her ability to parent her children. [The judge's statement in the trial transcript.]

In case US15 the judge viewed the difficulties with visitation, due to the mother's belief in her accusations against the father, as a clue to the mother's personality problems:

> This court views mother as a danger to the best interests of the three children if her conduct does not change. The relentless attack, by mother and her parents, on the father of these children, and his family, if it continued, is likely to do lasting damage to the young[children]. . . . Mother has pledged to this court that she would enter counseling. Without such material commitment, given the facts of this case, the court would not have awarded mother custody. [The current judge paraphrasing the former judge's comments regarding the mother's behavior.]

The mother in case US15 was given what would be paraphrased in the words of the court as "many chances" to improve her behavior in the earlier court decisions. The judges who had made the decisions in earlier court proceedings were reluctant to transfer custody because of the mother's role as primary caregiver. Eventually, however, the situation did not improve and residence and custody were transferred to the father.

In case US8 (the only case of a primary caregiver father) no basis was found by the professionals and experts involved in the case for any of the father's allegations against the mother. The accusations were viewed as an obvious fabrication, however, and led to less analysis by the experts and professionals regarding the father's mental health, although the accusations influenced the court's character assessment of the father to the extent that residence was transferred. In the US cases where a determination regarding the truth of an accusation was more difficult to ascertain, and where a parent refused to rethink her belief in the truth of the accusation (such as US31), the parent's negative character assessment by the court linked up with a negative assessment of the parent's personality by the professional or expert. The negative psychological assessment of a recalcitrant parent is linked in custody cases to the judges' role as *finders of fact*. The role of the court as *finders of fact* adds to the court's ability to create a particular version of truth; this is what will become the legally accepted version of the events of a case. In the US a parent acting in disbelief of this version of the truth is viewed similarly to a person who does not believe in reality. In other words, an unrepentant parent is described as either willful, with the understanding that the court knows that the parent is lying and yet the parent continues to lie, as in case US8, or the parent is viewed as being in a delusional state which involves the parent's incorrect interpretation of reality. That is to say, reality has been revealed to the parent by the court with the assistance of the professionals and experts and still the parent refuses to believe it. The judge in case US31 angrily expressed this idea to the mother in the excerpt below:

> While as you sit here and shake your head, if you would just stop and think logically and not emotionally for a minute about the self-righteousness arrogance that it takes to believe that you, as opposed to everyone else in the world, is right. [The judge's statement in the trial court minutes.]

In cases US12 and US8, a quick determination was made by the court that the accusations were unequivocally false due to lack of any evidence found by the custody evaluators or any of the other investigators. In both these cases, the judges and the evaluators assessed the claims made by the accusing parent to be *very* thinly veiled fabrications. The judge noted in case US12 that the stories mother told had no basis in fact:

> [T]hat he had masturbated in the presence of the child . . . that the [mother] claims that the [father] was irresponsible either with respect to the quality of child care that he provided their child and with respect to safety issues . . . are further not credible. [The judge's statement in the trial memorandum.]

The judge's character assessment of the father and the expert's evaluation of the father were used as one basis for determining that these allegations were simply not true. In other words, the court's character assessment of the father did not find any basis upon which to suspect the father in case US12 of being capable of the acts which the mother ascribed to him (mother made allegations of very outrageous and violent acts against her by father), and no other evidence such as police reports or hospital reports was offered by the mother to support her claims.[8]

There is an assumption that false allegations of sexual abuse are common and often arise in contested custody cases, in contrast to the possibility that allegations of sexual abuse might lead to contested custody cases. For instance, Mertz and Lonsway (1998, 1415-1437) found in their study that courts commonly believe that women falsely accuse their spouses of child sexual abuse in order to gain an advantage in divorce. Danforth and Welling (1996, 121) also found that "negative stereotypes about women encourage judges to disbelieve women's allegations of child sexual abuse against their child by former partners." The judge in case US15 echoes this commonly held understanding of such accusations:

> The court is disturbed by an undercurrent, that often rises to flood stage in cases as adversarial as this one, that father somehow, in some way, may have been physically inappropriate with [child]. The court rejects the innuendo and finds no credible evidence that such an incident occurred. [The judge's statement in the trial court memorandum.]

In both Swedish and US society there exists the idea that sexual abuse allegations are a sure way for an accusing parent to gain residence and custody in contested cases.[9] The US sample cases did not reflect such a notion (the Swedish cases had only a small number of these instances). Instead, an entrenched view regarding the validity of the accusation, by one parent against the other, worked against the parent making the accusation.[10] In all US cases in which such allegations were made, with the exception of two cases, one in which the accusations were deemed to be substantiated and the other where it was found the father did not actually want to have residential custody (US67), custody and residence was awarded or transferred to the parent who had been accused of the abuse. The substantiated case involved the testimony of an older child. Even in this substantiated case, however, the mother was viewed negatively by the judge and described as using the abuse allegations of the older child in a tactical way in order to keep the father from visiting with the two younger children.

Small innuendos of inappropriate behavior could also negatively impact on the character of the accusing parent. Perhaps, as suggested by the judge in case US15 above, there is the fear that lesser allegations will turn into more problematic allegations in the future. In case US11, for example, the mother did not accuse the father of sexually abusing the child but rather claimed that the nine-year-old child had disclosed to her an incident of inappropriate behavior (which was not detailed in the file) on the part of the father. The accusation was used to add weight by the court to other descriptions of this mother's character that described her as overly sensitive and nervous. Although the child had lived with her mother all her life and additionally lived with her mother during the two-year divorce process, sole custody and residence was awarded to the father. The claim by the mother of inappropriate behavior by the father tied in with the description of the mother's character and the idea that mother might not be a friendly parent. In contrast to the Swedish court, the US assessment of a parent's character as less than reasonable outweighs other considerations, such as the usual weight given to continuity of care. This is because reasonable action (such as encouraging visitation with the non-resident parent) on the part of a parent viewed as unreasonable by the court, cannot be or is not assumed by the court order alone.

A concentration on the personality and actions of individuals in the US cases helped to frame how allegations were interpreted by the judges and what part these allegations came to play in the court narrative. Where the allegations were considered untrue or embellished, they helped to create a picture of the accusing parent as the cause of the trouble of nonagreement. In other words, an individual was at the root of the trouble of nonagreement and the character assessment of this individual created a narrative that supported such a conclusion. In cases where there was more indecision regarding the validity of the allegation the judge's interpretation of the accusing parent could work similarly as in case US31. The mother in that case continued over a period of two years to hold her belief that the father had sexually abused their children. The custody evaluator reiterates the mother's position in the quote below:

> [Mother] views herself as the children's sole protector from, not only father, but a court system that has failed to act decisively on their behalf. She believes that by continuing to entertain father's claims of innocence of wrongdoing, and his requests for visitation, the court has permitted the stress of this custody dispute to continue unabated. [The family relations counselor's statement in the custody evaluation.]

The allegations were discussed by the psychological expert in the case as arising only in the mind of the mother. A closer look at the record, however, shows that one of the children first made claims regarding sexual abuse (by a person not determined) to doctors and other professionals. After one investigation, a doctor confirmed that the child had physical evidence of having been sexually abused. The evidence did not point to a *false* allegation but rather to a question of *who* was responsible for the abuse and if the mother, in her dislike for the father, merely assumed that he was the guilty person, and after having drawn that conclusion refused to be convinced of any alternative. Early in the case the family relations counselor's report contained a sense of indeterminacy regarding who was telling the truth and who was not:

> Given mother's stated belief that father is abusing [child], she under-standably is reluctant to allow him visitation with any of the children. Given father's stated belief that mother is emotionally unstable and strongly motivated to maintain her custodial status and remove him from the family residence and access to the children, he feels that the children are at risk in her care and in danger of being manipulated to make accusations against him. [The family relations counselor's statement in the custody evaluation.]

The mother's belief did not arise totally without basis. If the mother believed that her conclusions regarding the abuse were a possibility she had been supported, at least initially, by investigations which had concluded that there was positive evidence of abuse. In fact, it was not the mother who first raised the issue of sexual abuse but the father when he claimed that this same child had reported inappropriate behavior by a friend of the mother. After this incident, the father and mother tried to reconcile. Shortly after this, however, the child made new allegations and statements to child protection workers in which the child claimed inappropriate behavior by a few different individuals, including the father. No charges were made against any individual. Nevertheless, at this point the mother broke off reconciliation and became convinced that the father was the person responsible for the child's claims of abuse. Nowhere in the record was it discussed what specific reasons the mother might have for being so sure that the father was the perpetrator of this abuse rather than another person who might have had access to the child. Instead, such omissions work to give to the narrative of the court and the psychological expert the idea that mother's allegations were tactical and that, if abuse had taken place it was not the father who was responsible. The judge based this assessment on the character assessment of the father and the lack of any evidence pointing specifically to the father by child protection services or the expert evaluator. The psychological evaluation, however, was unlikely to result in any conclusive proof of guilt or lack of guilt by the father as it took place long after the initial allegations (and there had not been any contact between father and children during that time). Furthermore, it involved psychological tests unlikely to be useful in the assessment of whether or not father had committed the abuse. The record mentions that the mother described the father as abusive in their relationship. The mother also related how she had repeatedly tried to reconcile with the father until the child made the accusations regarding the abuse at which point the mother cut off all contact with her former husband. Due to the sexual abuse allegations, the father did not see the children for two years after the parents' last attempt at reconciliation. He was given supervised visitation during this period, but he did not attend the visits with his children. The family relations counselor was critical of the father's lack of contact with the children over this period of time, stating:

> [R]eportedly [father] . . . has sent no correspondence, made no calls, nor sent any presents to his children for two and one-half years. He has been advised for over two years that it would be in his best interest to substantiate his position through psychological evaluation, and has not done so. [The family relations counselor.]

In contrast, the court did not follow the questioning tone of the family relations counselor regarding why the father did not follow through with the supervised visitation or why the father refused during this period to pay child support. The court narrative related a story which viewed these factors as being caused by the mother. According to the court the mother's insistence on the reality of abuse had led to the supervised visitation with the implied idea that the father could not follow through in maintaining such a limited relationship with his children. Instead, the father's behavior was framed by the judge in semi-heroic terms:

> [D]ad while he has shortcomings, has done a yeoman's job of taking difficult situation and putting tremendous effort and concern in it. I can not overstate, given all the cases that I see, how unusual it is for someone so many years after allegations, difficulty, and estrangement to bring the degree of dedication, that he has to trying to restore the relationship that he has with his kids. It speaks volumes. [The judge's statement in the trial transcript.]

Since we know the father did not try to contact the children via the GAL or the family relations counselor to send gifts or letters, nor did he attempt to attend his scheduled supervised visitation, the acts of dedications to which the court refers must implicitly refer to the fact that he did not drop the custody process. The judge's narrative could have followed a different narrative line than it did. For example, the actions of the father after he was accused by the mother may have been viewed negatively for the father. The court could have developed a story of parental irresponsibility and lack of care using the father's lack of visiting and not paying anything toward the support of the children as evidence of this lack of care. However, the narrative frame used in the US cases, which views an individual as the problem, created a picture of the mother as the cause of conflict. Father was the injured party and his actions, including his lack of action, were depicted as heroic.

Custody of the two youngest children, including the one who made the allegations, was transferred to the father. The oldest child was judged to be too aligned with the mother to be ordered to live with the father. After the transfer of custody, the mother claimed that the other child, who had been placed in father's care, also made allegations against the father. This alleged revelation on the part of this child prompted mother to take the child to a specialist, during the time they were visiting with her, to see if specialist could confirm the abuse (abuse could not be confirmed). The point of this review of the US court narrative in cases where there are allegations and trouble with visitation is not to stress that the US court made the wrong decision, but to understand other ways of viewing conflict which may have resulted in differing narratives in these cases. Were alternative narratives in which one parent is not held solely responsible for the conflict possible in the US cases reviewed here? Or was the outcome of these cases as self-evident as the judges' narratives imply? In answer to this we can compare a few similar cases in the Swedish sample. It is important to note that the number of cases in which sexual allegations are mentioned as part of the narrative in the Swedish sample is very small.[11] There were three cases in which accusations of sexual abuse had any part in the court or social worker's narrative (SW7, SW26 and SW18). Case SW26 contained allegations of sexual abuse. In SW7 the mother made an innuendo that the father might have done something to frighten the child while the child was in the father's care (SW7 is discussed more fully in chapter 5). In case SW26, the accusing parent was the nonresident mother. The father brought the case to court to try and get sole custody of the children because of the accusations made against him by the mother (the parents had, at the time of the process, joint residential custody). The social report noted these allegations, but did not analyze the validity of the allegations in any depth in the case records. The court did not mention them. Sole residence with the child was awarded to the father. The court supported its conclusion for sole residence by referring to the fact that mother's residence in the children's familiar environment might be in jeopardy as she was threatened with eviction. The third case (SW18) involved the deterioration of the father's visiting time with his sons after he was convicted of the sexual assault of another child. The court was not critical of either of the parents' personalities, or of the events which had led to the deteriorating relationship between the father and his children. At the same time, the court was determined that the situation should improve and that the relationship between the father and children be revived. Even in case SW18, where blame may have easily been ascribed to the father (he was convicted of a crime against a child) or the mother (she may have been viewed as acting tactically regarding the father's conviction), the Swedish court did not connect these actions to an assessment of the character of the parents. Instead, the actions were viewed as the reason for the breakdown of the parents' partnership and communication which needed time and understanding to be reestablished. The mother was expected to develop trust in the father again given the gradually increasing time schedule for visiting put in place by the court. The father was expected to be understanding of the mother's need to regain trust in him as the father of the children. Even when serious allegations were involved, the Swedish court viewed the trouble as a misunderstanding that could be overcome by each parent's acknowledgment of the other parent's point of view. The reasons for the conflict did not equal a reason for noncooperation, in the view of the Swedish court. The reasons for the conflict were made clear so that the parents would be made aware of where the problems existed so they could work on their misunderstanding. There is an implicit understanding in this view of the parents as reasonable people. However, as is seen in case SW26, whatever might not fit in with the view of conflict as misunderstanding can simply be left outside the frame. So that, for example, to what extent the mother's sexual abuse accusation in case SW26 may have led to the sole custody determination for the father was not engaged with explicitly by either the social report writers or the judges making the decision in the case.

In the case of the US there is no way of knowing whether or not the US judges made mistakes in their *finding of fact* in any of the cases where custody was transferred. The sexual allegation cases analyzed in this chapter show that when serious allegations are made in the US, one parent is viewed as the cause of the trouble, either the accusing parent refuses to accept what the court regards as the truth (that no abuse took place) or if the allegations are substantiated what the result of that knowledge should be. It can be conjectured, perhaps, that when a parent is viewed by the court as guilty of the abuse then that parent would be viewed as the cause of the trouble. None of the sample cases, however, contained such a narrative even when the abuse was considered substantiated, as in case US45.

NOTES

1. For further criteria in Connecticut regarding continuity of care see *Cappetta v. Cappetta*, 196 Conn. 10, 16, 490 A.2d 996 (1985). And also Ginzberg, 1995 and Kramer, 1994. The court can make any decision it regards as in the best interest of the child. Nonetheless, when the courts decided against awarding residence to the primary-caregiver the court seemed to want to prove clear and strong reasons for that choice.

2. *Giles v. Giles,* 2003 WL 1818006 (Minn. App. April 8, 2003) (unpublished).

3. *White v. Kimrey,* 847 So.2d 157, 37,408 (La. App. 2 Cir. 5/14/03).

4. The perception of the actors, in Sweden, regarding this gentle criticism may be stronger than such criticism would be to US participants.

5. Föräldrabalken 6 kap. § 15.

6. The visitation being discussed was a week of residential custody once a month.

7. In one of the two cases where allegations were made in the Swedish sample, the visiting parent made the allegation (SW26).

8. I am not doubting that some individuals are capable of outrageous acts of violence, however nothing from either case US8 or US12 pointed to ambiguity in the judges' assessments of the events.

9. Some studies drew big conclusions from small samples, and contributed to the idea that sexual abuse allegations were rampant in contested custody cases, for example Schuman 1986, 5-20; Green 1986, 449; and Benedek and Schetky 1984. Although now dated and widely debunked, these studies are still continually referenced in support of the myth of rampant false allegations of child sexual abuse in custody disputes. Ideas regarding the prevalence of widespread false child sexual abuse allegations can be attributed, at least in part, to Richard Gardner and his theory of parental alienation syndrome. A service industry has sprung up in reference to the idea of the prevalence of false allegations. See, for example: False Allegations.com http://www.false-allegations.com/sommerbio.html (accessed June 21, 2008.) This site offers expert services for parents involved in custody conflicts where allegations have been made.

10. For studies on the validity of child sexual abuse allegations in divorce see Humphreys 1997, 529; Thoennes and Tjaden 1990, 151-63; and Penfold 1997, 11-30. In an Australian study it was concluded that the percentage of false child abuse (for all types of abuse) reports in custody and visitation cases was the same as in child protection services. However, the number of child abuse reports in custody visitation cases had gone up between the years 1993-1997. Nine percent of abuse reports were judged

to be false, the same as in the child protection register (Brown, Frederico, Hewitt, and Sheehan 2000, 849-859). Also see Bala and Schuman 2000, 191-241. The Bala and Schuman study concluded that judges found fathers were more likely to make false charges of abuse (of all types of abuse, not just sexual). Mothers' accusations were deemed intentionally false by civil courts in 1.3 percent of cases compared with 21 percent of fathers' accusations. Additionally, the research found that in a judicial finding on the balance of probabilities (the civil standard) that abuse occurred was made in 46 cases (23 percent of all cases). In 89 cases, the judges made a finding that the allegations were unfounded. In a further 61 cases there was evidence of abuse but no judicial conclusion that abuse occurred. In 45 of the 150 cases (30 percent of the cases where abuse was not substantiated) the judge believed that it was an intentionally false allegation (including both mothers and fathers).

11. The same myth regarding the commonplace occurrence of such allegations is present in Sweden (Svensson 2003). This newspaper article discusses the idea common in both Sweden and the US that mothers often use false accusations of incest or domestic violence against fathers to keep fathers away from their children.

FOUR

Professionals and Experts in Sweden and the US

This chapter asks how the representatives of knowledge, in both the US and Sweden, collect evidence and interpret the events of a case. The US and Swedish representatives of knowledge can be compared in terms of knowledge as *expertise* versus knowledge as the *technique of empathy*. These different approaches to knowledge in Sweden and the US result in differing interpretations regarding the actions of the parents.

TWO TECHNIQUES IN THE USE OF KNOWLEDGE

Both Sweden and the US make use of psychological knowledge in contested cases but in radically different ways. US society focuses the problem of nonagreement and conflict on individuals; from this viewpoint knowledge is directed or complemented by the use of psychology which describes individuals in terms of their personalities. The understanding of conflict within US society as something that is caused by individuals directs custody evaluations toward describing individuals as particular types of people and defining the personalities of actors in order to determine the cause (person or persons) of the conflict. Searching for answers to the impasse between two parents along such lines becomes reinforcing of the view of conflict as caused by individuals; a view of conflict caused by individuals is confirmed by focusing on personalities from which the problem of conflict is said to arise. The best interest of the child definition, according to the representatives of knowledge in the US, lies in identifying the individual who is at the bottom of the conflict through testing and psychological evaluation. In Sweden the problem is viewed as a problem of relationships. Psychology provides a method, the basis of

47

which is *empathy*, for drawing out the feelings of the participants in order for the professional to draw attention to the source of their misunderstanding. The evaluation process is used as a way of finding out where the misunderstandings between the pair are located in order to help them end their relationship problem and to come to an agreement which would alleviate the necessity for the court to decide what the definition of best interest would be.

In the US cases, psychological knowledge tended to frame mother's negative behavior as irrational and dangerous and father's negative behavior as bad but rational action. When mothers' actions were viewed as irrational in the US sample, mothers were perceived to be a threat to their children. In contrast, the bad behavior of fathers was explainable or taken for granted and considered within the normal range of male action. In Sweden framing the problem as a misunderstanding resulted in the downplaying of information that did not lend itself to this understanding of the situation. It also led to the assumption that both parents were equal in their capability of bringing about a compromise. Characterizations of the parents were less gendered in the Swedish case. Nevertheless, the way of framing the problem as one of mutual conflict, coupled with the value of compromise, can if it does not allow reflection on power imbalances or violence in a relationship lead to one parent merely giving in to the demands of the dominant parent.

PSYCHOLOGICAL KNOWLEDGE AND EXPERTISE IN THE US

The dependence upon psychological experts in legal proceedings more generally in US courtrooms has led to the development of psychological experts who specialize in presenting evidence to a court. This development has led to a field of forensic psychology in which experts give evidence, make reports and testify in court but whose main area of expertise is not knowledge of attachment theory, child development or child psychology. It is possible, for example, to receive a Ph.D. in forensic psychology. That psychological recommendations are not rendered more often by child specialists is an indication of what is considered to be the source of the problem in the US cases. The type of psychology used in the US cases focuses on individuals. In other words, psychology is used to interpret the personalities of the parents (and sometimes the children) and to analyze the parents' claims and actions against this psychological interpretation. The methods used by experts favor tests and assessments that seem to be carried out in an objective manner; that is, the expert should not have a prior therapeutic relationship with any of the people being evaluated. In this way, the evaluations are viewed as providing an objective narrative of the participants' personalities and interpretation of the participants' claims; such psychological assessment, therefore, coincides with the idea of fairness which is inherent in rational legal processes. The objective quality of the procedures used to carry out these evaluations imbues them with the aura that the assessments are in some sense scientific.

The pervasiveness of the type of psychological knowledge that is used to define individual personalities in the US has begun to be used even by the professional social workers carrying out custody evaluations who are not highly trained in the application of such knowledge. In other words, the custody evaluators also write in the language of personalities derived from psychology, as will be shown in chapter 5. In some jurisdictions in the US, trained psychologists have taken over all the functions of social work custody evaluators (Bowermaster 2002, 265).[1] Custody evaluators, both experts and professionals, now commonly approach their target populations with particular types of psychological frames derived from the type of psychological knowledge contained in expert evaluations, even before the frames are linked to specific individuals. As noted custody evaluator Stahl opines:

> Many custody evaluators observe that most high-conflict families have one or both parents who exhibit narcissistic, obsessive-compulsive, histrionic, paranoid, or borderline features. (1999, 8-16)

Twenty-nine cases out of the 67 US cases included a report, ordered by the court, carried out by a psychological evaluator.[2] The psychological evaluation report was done in addition to the family relations counselor's custody report, as in case US8 below:

> As a part of this matter, the parties participated in an evaluation by a Family Relations Counselor and, also, a psychological evaluation which included psychological testing, clinical interviews and clinical observation of each parent's interaction with [the child]. [The judge's statement in the trial court memorandum.]

Psychological evaluations include standardized personality tests, which have become a key component of the psychological investigator's method in US custody cases. Most of the tests administered by these psychological experts were developed for a clinical population, and the language used for the test indicates a concentration on such a population (Shuman 2002, 135). The tests frame the interpretation of parents' claims and actions through clinical language which uses, in an objective way, words that are laden with meaning. The phrase "the possibility of delusional thinking," for example, is used in the psychological evaluation of the case *Breitenfeldt v. Nickles-Breitenfeldt,* cited below:

> The MMPI-2 suggests use of paranoid defenses, resulting in misinterpretations of others' motives, rigidity in her thoughts and actions, rationalizing her own behavior, and denying her own negative motives. The possibility of delusional thinking is suggested. In interpersonal

relationships she is likely to be intense, emotional, controlling and demanding. [The judge paraphrasing evidence from the psychological test results.][3]

The testing language itself imbues a sense of gravity to the conclusions made about the individuals in the cases through the choice of words that are *standard phrases* used in the tests. The psychological descriptors of the parents given by the testing language may not even be visible in the parents' actions outside of the testing situation. The psychological expert in *McKechnie v. McKechnie* admitted on cross-examination that mother was not exhibiting any signs of psychosis, even though the language of the tests used to describe her made it appear as though she was:

> In his report, the custody evaluator recommended that the trial court grant the father sole legal custody, institute joint counseling for the mother and their daughter, and limit the mother's visitation. He reported that psychological testing revealed that the mother had "a paranoid personality makeup with a currently borderline or overtly psychotic state." However, at the hearing, the custody evaluator admitted that he had difficulty "during his evaluation process in being able to 'get a handle' on what was really happening in this case." On cross-examination, he retracted certain statements included in his report as being without support. He also admitted that testing can falsely indicate paranoia if the test subject feels threatened. He noted that the mother exhibited no traits of psychosis.[4]

In *McKechnie v. McKechnie* the appeals court affirmed the trial court's decision not to award father sole custody and reduce the mother's visitation as the above psychological evaluator had recommended. Psychological knowledge, as it is used by both the experts and professionals in the US cases, sometimes creates a story of probabilities. That is to say, the evaluator claims to find evidence of a particular aspect of concern in a parent's personality and the evaluator claims that this feature will lead to something negative for the child. Such speculation can be damaging for the parent against whom it is made. It was the predictive quality of the evaluation in *Donald v. Donald*, below, that led to the dissenting opinion of one of the appeals court judges:

> The trial court was strongly influenced by C's evaluation of the parties; indeed, it seems that C's testimony might have determined the outcome. C's evaluation was essentially a set of predictions of future behavior. Based on her assessment tools, C predicted that plaintiff would fail to recognize the child's needs and put them before her own. This prediction is not, however, corroborated by anything plaintiff actually did or did not do.[5]

The plaintiff was, nonetheless, unsuccessful in her appeal, so that predictions of future parental action, even when not based on past behavior, were viewed as a valid way for a custody evaluator to define the best interest of the child. This feature of psychological evaluation can interact with the tendency of children's interests to be viewed in terms of children as a *potential*, as described in the introduction. A child, as in the case above, may express the desire to live with the negatively described parent. However, when children are viewed as having a greater interest attached to the adult person that they will become, rather than the person they presently are, a child will have to be protected from the negatively described parent's potential for particular actions.

Psychological evaluations and the language which is produced from such evaluations work together with the character assessment of the trial court which is a characterization of the parents based on the legal conception of what is held to be a reasonable or unreasonable person. This becomes linked to the idea of a rational/irrational personality arising from the psychological evaluation, particularly where a decision will be made against residence for the primary caregiver or the current resident parent. In *Kirk v. Kirk* the judge paraphrases in the character assessment the psychological expert's observations of the parents' personalities:

> [Father] was diagnosed as recently as October 2000 as having a "chip on his shoulder". . . . He is "narcissistically disturbed" and at least as concerned with his own image and presentation as he is with his daughter's well-being. [Mother] has her own issues. She was diagnosed as "severely narcissistically disordered" and "unknowingly involved in manipulative, deceitful and exploitative behaviors in an effort to preserve her pathological enmeshment with her daughter."[6]

Both parents' personalities are judged harshly in the above quote. However, there is a subtle elevation of the mother's negative personality traits; she is "severely narcissistically disordered" in contrast to father's being "narcissistically disturbed." Having a "chip on one's shoulder" does not sound pathological. The "unknowing" quality of mother's "manipulative and deceitful and exploitative behaviors and enmeshment" does. Enmeshment is a particularly laden psychological term to use for the description of a parent-child psychological relationship. When applied to mothers, the term "enmeshment" produces images of the flip side of sentimentalized maternal love. Additionally, it seems to implicitly require that the parent who is so enmeshed be disentangled from their child, thus producing a call for action. When individuals are the focus of the source of conflict, psychological evaluations carried out by experts, along with evaluations of professionals that proceed from a view of psychology that defines individuals, lend validity to a particular kind of interpretation of the actors and their actions in the cases, namely as potentially pathological and irrational.

PSYCHOLOGY AS EMPATHETIC TECHNIQUE IN SWEDEN

The role of the Swedish state in providing a basic standard of care for its citizens, as typified by the Swedish social democratic welfare regime, and by extension the necessity of the state in providing for the well-being of its citizens, is directly related to the role of the Swedish social worker. It relates to the way in which social workers carry out their tasks of custody evaluation, what criteria they look at, and the legitimacy given to their conclusions by the tingsrätt. The Swedish focus on problems in the relationship between people creates a situation in which all the participants in the conflict should have a chance to be listened to. In the custody and visitation conflict, psychology is not used by Swedish social workers to define or explain individuals, but as a technique for listening to all the participants in the conflict. Being a listener demonstrates the caring role performed by the Swedish state through its representative, the social worker, and yet such care can also involve a repressive element in that there are few ways for the participants to challenge the conclusions of the report writers. There were no other experts or professional recommendations in the Swedish cases. Participants in the Swedish cases are viewed as normal people and so the professional social worker's judgment of the issues involved in the case is viewed as the appropriate one for the task. Namely, the Swedish social worker's role as the representative of the knowledge of care gives the social worker the legitimacy to judge aspects of care and the interactions and misunderstandings between people. The custody report writers are assumed, by the Swedish tingsrätt, to have the necessary professional knowledge to evaluate relationship difficulties between people and assess the problems of lack of cooperation that arise from these relationship difficulties.

The idea of the "frame analysis of talk," discussed by Goffman, is apt when describing the professional technique used by Swedish report writers for gathering information about a case. Goffman proposed that "a tale or anecdote," what he termed a "replaying," was not simply the reporting of a past event:

> In the fullest sense, it . . . is a statement couched from the personal perspective of an actual or potential participant who is located so that some temporal, dramatic development of the reported event proceeds from that starting point. A replaying will therefore, incidentally, be something that listeners can empathetically insert themselves into vicariously re-experiencing what took place. (1986, 504)

The Swedish report writers present a "replaying." Their reports recount the personal experiences of the parents' relationship (and sometimes also the children's account) in the words of the parents; they do not just report on the events that are being recalled (Goffman 1986, 504). This facet exemplifies the Swedish social worker's attempt to unlock the story of the conflict by reproducing the parental narratives and the link these re-counted narratives have with empathy. "Replaying" as opposed to "re-porting" produces a situation of empathy, in which the social report writ-ers become empathetic listeners and not merely evidence gatherers. The purpose of the evaluation in the Swedish case is not just the resulting recommendation, but also to have everyone be understood and empa-thized with in an effort to uncover the misunderstanding between the people involved. Candace Clark's theories regarding sympathy are rele-vant in this context. In Clark's thesis, sympathy (of which empathy can be viewed as an extension) is "an emotion that we perform. In the act of empathy, one takes on the role of the other in order to understand them." Emotional resources, such as empathy, are given "with the expectation that other resources will be given back" (2005, 56-63). In the present situa-tion the expectation is that when the two stories (one from each parent) are made available, in the form of the completed report to the conflicted participants, the disclosures along with the participants' perceptions that they have been understood (empathized with) will lead to a compromise. Clark posits that modern culture has led to the expansion of acceptable situations in which individuals can be the recipients of sympathy. This has led to the creation of professionals she views as sympathy entrepren-eurs, that is to say, professional sympathizers (Clark 2005, 56-63). Swed-ish professional empathizers cannot be thought of as sympathy entre-preneurs due to the relationship between the state and its responsibility for the distribution of care. Instead, Swedish custody evaluators are the distributors of state-sponsored empathy and the care expected of a social democratic welfare regime (Holm 2001, 53-75). Also, the report-writing professional cannot strictly be said to be neutral; to be neutral suggests a standing back from feeling in order to be objective, as the psychological evaluators in the US cases aim to be. In contrast, the Swedish report writer's aim is to feel with each of the participants equally so that all the participants are understood and feel that they are are understood through being listened to by the professional empathizers. The empathet-ic technique and listening are closely linked, for one cannot understand or feel for another unless the professional hears that other person. The report writer's questions are meant to elicit the parties' thoughts and feelings regarding the situation and to get to know them as a way of discovering the solution to the misunderstanding. One of the ways this is apparent in the Swedish cases is verbatim reporting of what the parents or children have said during the interview. Where the US cases tended to paraphrase what the parents said, the Swedish reports contained natural-sounding repetitions of what the parents said in response to the report writers' (unstated) questions. The questions used were evident from the responses of the parents and the similarity of the responses of the parents across the cases. Common prompts, for example, included: "tell me something about your childhood?" "How did you meet the parent of your child?" "What was your relationship like in the beginning?" "How did it end?" "What is your life like now?" In case SW38, for example, the mother described her youth:

> Mother was raised in [town] together with her parents and two older brothers. She describes her youth as sometimes good and sometimes bad. [Mother's statement recorded by the custody evaluator in the custody evaluation.]

In another case the father was asked about his hobbies and social network:

> In his free time he likes to be with his children. He says that he has too much time on his hands. He has many interests and likes to take long walks and to be out on a boat, or to dance. [The father's statement in the custody evaluation.] Case SW2

There was almost always the response by the parents to the request: "Describe your child." In case SW30, for example, the father answered this question by saying:

> [He] likes to mess around with fixing cars and he likes animals. He likes to do things together with his daddy. He likes to be the center of attention and needs a lot of attention. He is patient and can have a lot of concentration when he is doing something he is interested in. [Father's statement in the custody evaluation.]

The purpose of the Swedish reports was not simply the production of a report but the therapeutic value of the parents and children talking about themselves. There was, however, no psychological analysis of the content of the interviews in terms evaluating the participants' personalities. There were no definitions of people as psychological types or of having particular psychological characteristics. Although psychology, in terms of the professional application of the technique of empathy, was used to elicit the participants' feelings, the report writer did not try to interpret the parents' individual psyches based upon the parents' expression of these feelings. The language of the reports were kept distinctly colloquial. Clichéd references to various feeling states were mentioned. A parent or child might be referred to as "feeling good about themselves" or "feeling bad about themselves." In the case below, for example, the mother describes how she feels:

> [Mother] . . . said that she feels tired, worn out and alone in caring for the child. [Mother's statement in the custody evaluation.] Case SW48

Intervention by mental health experts was not part of the legal dispute process in any of the Swedish sample cases. There was one psychological interview, carried out in case SW16. However, the credentials of this psychologist were found to be inappropriate for the case and so none of the expert's conclusions were included in either the final custody evaluation or in the court order. Participants might be involved in contact with mental health care professionals separately from the court process, as in case SW23. However, there were no recommendations, in any of the cases, made by a mental health provider regarding the type of custody or frequency of visitation. In case SW23, for example, the mother was suffering from a mental illness. The mother's mental health issues preceded the custody process. The doctors involved in mother's mental health care did not make recommendations regarding what decision should be made in the tingsrätt trial.[7] None of the Swedish custody reports suggested a course of therapeutic intervention for the parents or children as a condition of the recommendation. The language of the Swedish custody evaluations was rarely critical of one parent over the other. Compare this semblance of balance with the bitingly critical tone of the custody evaluator in *Donald v. Donald* excerpt below. In the excerpt from a US appeals court case, the dissenting appeals court judge noted the following regarding the tone of the custody evaluator:

> [Custody evaluator's] contemptuous attitude toward [mother] is apparent from reading the transcript. For example, [custody evaluator] all but recommended termination of [mother's] parental rights by opining that the child should not be placed with [mother] even if [father] were not available to take custody. It is therefore not surprising that [mother] would be evasive and defensive when dealing with [custody evaluator].[8]

The natural language of the Swedish reports, nevertheless, made it more difficult to discern whether what was attributed to the parents and children was actually an interpretation of the report writer of what a participant had said or a verbatim statement of what was said during the interview. Similarly, the ways in which a report writer might sway the report to give a more negative impression of one of the parents were more difficult to assess. This chapter now turns to look at how the two different focuses of knowledge seen in the US and Sweden impacted on the story that the professionals and experts in both countries provided to the court about the parents and the children.

FATHERS' BAD ACTIONS AND IRRATIONAL MOTHERS IN THE US

In a process where the problem of conflict is viewed as one between individuals, knowledge is used to define individuals and produces descriptions of some actions as irrational and the parents carrying out those actions as mentally unhealthy. There is a gender divide in psychological descriptions; fathers' actions were more likely to be viewed as within a normal range of male actions, whereas when mothers' negative actions came under analysis they were viewed through psychological frames which defined mothers as mentally unhealthy or potentially mentally unhealthy. The gendered idea of action as it relates to categorization of mental health has been discussed by Busfield. She writes:

> [E]xaggerations of masculinity have often tended to be defined not as mental disorder but as delinquency: that is, they may be viewed as unacceptable but not as raising questions of possible psychological disorder . . . there has been something of an asymmetry in the response to male and female exaggerations: problematic female behaviours have tended to be viewed as mental disorder; problematic male behaviours as evidence of wrongdoings. (1996, 104)

As Busfield (106-107) notes, it is the idea of agency and rationality which, in part, underscores the gendered view of what is described as "a problem of mental health" versus the understanding of action as "problematic behavior." "Rationality" she says, " is highly valued in modern societies, [and] is central to the concept of mental disorder—indeed, it is through its opposition with rationality that the concept takes on its meaning. But like agency, assumptions of rationality are not independent of gender" (106-107). Inherent ideas of masculinity, Busfield claims, view masculinity as "active" and as implying agency and rationality, whereas ideas of the feminine imply "passivity" and a lack of agency and hence irrational action, because one does not plot out or is not mindful of acting if one is denied agency (106-107). In the circumstances of custody and visitation conflicts in the US the particular understanding regarding the role of mothers and fathers interacts with features of what is acceptable male or female behavior. Ideas about the role of mother in the US, as shown in the weight given to the criteria of continuity of care in the US cases, are influenced by assumptions regarding a mother's role in the emotional development of her child. This focus, often implicit, is founded on theories that are derived from psychoanalytical theory and ideas such as *the psychological parent* encapsulated in the thesis of Goldstein, Freud and Solnit (1984). In contrast, the understanding of the crucial and unique role of fathers, in the US, is linked with socialization theory. Socialization theory renders father absence the most crucial negative aspect of the father-child relationship, rather than, for example, violence and abuse. From the US point of view, children need continuity of care provided by mother due to her role as *the* unique psychological parent who has the key formative role in a child's psychological development. It is just this unique role, however, which puts mother's actions under greater scrutiny in contested cases. The unique role given to mother-caregiver is compounded by the gendered aspect involved in the interpretation of women's and men's actions. Both mother and father might be viewed as the root of the problem of nonagreement in the US cases. Yet the way in which women's actions were framed as irrational, and men's actions framed as bad behavior, led to a division in how their personalities were described to the court and influenced the recommendations made by both the experts and professionals in the cases.

The framing of mothers' personalities as irrational can be separated from those cases where explicit instances of psychosis were a factor in one parent asking for a transfer of custody, such as in case US65 below:

> Mother was admitted to a Hospital psychiatric unit from [dates]. Father became concerned when his wife claimed to be receiving messages from a radio station and the home computer and called the police and paramedics. The mother's principal diagnosis on admission was reactive psychosis. [The judge's statement in the trial court memorandum.]

In contrast to US65, other cases defining mother's actions as irrational did not involve visible psychosis on the part of the mother. Nonetheless, an image was created, through the use of psychological language to describe mother's bad behavior, of a parent who was potentially harmful to her children's psychological health. This is especially true for those mothers who carried out actions that were out of the gendered realm of female action, for example when a mother exhibited aggressive, loud, strident or abusive behavior. Mother's negative actions were viewed as indicative of an irrational person; it is understood that such an irrational individual cannot take part in cooperative action and therefore must be viewed as the cause of continuing conflict. This was seen, for example, in case US13, discussed in chapter 3.

In contrast, fathers' negative actions were less likely to be viewed as an indication of psychological problems, and if such actions were used to describe a father's personality, they were unlikely to be linked to the father's care for his children. In case US30, the father engaged in destructive activities. He was aggressive and verbally abusive toward the mother. It was noted by the judge that he may have tried to have the mother assaulted or killed. He unequivocally told the custody evaluator he hoped that "the bitch die[s]." Despite the father's words and actions, a psychological evaluation of the father was not viewed as necessary. In fact, overlooking the father's possible attempts on the mother's life, the GAL recommended that residential custody be transferred to the father. This was despite the fact that the primary caregiver mother had been and remained a suitable carer for the children. In contrast to the GAL, the judge viewed the father's behavior as bad and did not transfer custody to him. The court order reduced the father's visitation time but did not order that the time be supervised, nor did the judge suggest that the father needed therapy.[9]

In contrast, in cases where a mother was violent or aggressive, psychological examinations were ordered and carried out before the trial commenced. For example, in case US29 the mother became aggressive after custody of the child was transferred to the father in an earlier trial. Her aggressiveness was described through a frame of irrational and out of control emotions, requiring therapeutic intervention in addition to supervised visitation:

> Dr. [name] testified that at the present time, the [mother's] stress and frustration levels are causing her to regress to a point where she loses the ability to control herself fully, make rational decisions. . . . His recommendation is that the [mother] receive counseling from an experienced therapist and that her visitation be supervised until she is more in control. The court finds . . . there is no question whatsoever that unsupervised visitation between the [mother] and [child] is not in the child's best interests in light of the [mother's] present volatile, emotional and irrational state. Without supervision and therapeutic intervention, the [mother's] behavior will eventually put [child] at further, serious risk. [The psychological evaluator's testimony in the trial memorandum.]

The mother was not abusive to the child. She had been the child's primary caregiver for most of the child's life. Custody had been transferred to the father because the mother made visitation between the father and child difficult and because she was verbally abusive toward the father. In case US29 the court reiterated the idea of the mother's loss of control and ordered supervised visitation:

> [S]he has risked injury to herself, the [father], [child] and possibly innocent bystanders by the reckless operation of her motor vehicle. . . . Her anger and bitterness against the [father] and her frustration with the judicial process have so consumed her that she has lost the capacity to make rational judgments. [The judge's statement in the trial court memorandum.]

Case US29 can be compared with case US5 in which the father was verbally abusive, although it was not clear in the court narrative if he was violent. However, there was one action by the mother which was telling in this regard. In a protective gesture the mother had taken the father's handguns with her when she left the house at the time of the couple's separation. Additionally, the father had engaged in behavior that might have led to more questions being asked regarding his thought processes. He had extorted a custody agreement from the mother by holding the child hostage. This involved not letting the child out of his house to go to school or to see the mother until the mother signed an agreement for 50/50 residential custody. Neither supervised visitation for the father nor sole custody for the mother was recommended by the custody evaluator. Instead, joint custody and a visiting schedule for what amounted to joint residence was recommended. The family relations counselor suggested:

> [That] the parties be awarded joint legal custody with final decision making authority with the mother and that primary physical custody be given to the mother. The report recommends that the father be given visitation three weekends per month and one weekday per week. [The

family relations counselor's statement in the custody evaluation.] Case US5

In case US58 the father was asking for sole custody and the mother was asking for joint legal custody. The father was abusive toward the mother, and verbally abusive toward the children. The mother's involvement in a church that the father did not approve of had led him to start divorce proceedings against her. The children were angry with their father for his behavior and were becoming more aligned (according to the report) with both the mother and the teachings of her church. Neither of the parents in case US58 was evaluated positively. The father was found to be harassing and threatening toward the mother, as well as being aggressive, frightening, and demeaning toward the children. Nevertheless, the father's behavior was viewed as within the normal range of male action, not condoned but also not characterized as irrational. The family relations counselor, for example, described an incident of the father's abusive behavior:

> He slapped a fist near her face, awoke her throughout the night and poured water on her. He told her he would "break [her] f * * * skull in."
> [The family relations counselor's statements in the custody evaluation.]

Despite this statement of violent action, father's behavior was characterized as somewhat understandable considering the stress he was under (the stress arising from mother's religious beliefs). Additionally, the father could not be considered irrational because, in the words of the psychological evaluator, "he knows what appropriate behavior is." The negative assessment of the father arose from the fact that, given this understanding of appropriate anger, he still allowed himself to act aggressively. Meanwhile, the overall assessment of his personality as a rational person (bright and articulate) was left intact:

> The father has significant difficulty controlling his anger around the mother and the boys. He yells and calls names. His name-calling is harsh and biting. The father is bright and articulate. While he knows what is inappropriate behavior, despite counseling, the father lacks sufficient internal control to stop it, particularly when he is under stress. [The judge's paraphrasing of the psychological evaluation.]

In case US58 the mother's care for the children was not in question; she was not found to be abusive or neglectful. However, the psychological report's description of the mother paints a picture of her thought processes as irrational and the overall description of her personality by the psychologist as delusional:

> She is so focused upon how father is immoral and ungodly, that she clearly lost focus on what is in the boys' best interest during the divorce dispute. "This lack of insight is likely because her thinking regarding [her church] was found [by the psychological evaluator] to be irrational

and at times delusional." [The judge quoting the psychologist's evaluation report.]

The mother's behavior might have been analyzed differently perhaps as having been induced by a shocked reaction to the father's actions considering her strongly held religious beliefs. The father, for example, brought prostitutes to the family home, and was careless about leaving inappropriate sexually explicit web pages opened in view of the children. The evaluator recommended that the children live with the mother as he felt that they were the most accustomed to her care. In part, this recommendation was made due to the father's aggressiveness toward the children. That the psychological evaluator analyzed the father's actions as rational and the mother's actions as irrational is seen in the recommendation that this evaluator made in the case. The evaluator recommended, in a plan that hearkened back to when mothers were given the practical care of young children but fathers were legal guardians, that the father have final decision-making authority in all major decisions regarding the children. In other words, the evaluator recommended that the children live with the mother, but that the father be legally entitled to make all important decisions regarding their care. The judge did not follow this recommendation and instead ordered joint custody with residence to the mother. The children were under court order to not attend the mother's church.

In the US cases, both parents' behavior can be evaluated negatively and either parent may be viewed as responsible for the conflict; however, the use of the type of psychological knowledge that is employed in the US has a gendered quality in terms of the best interest standard. This is due to the fact that when mothers' actions are evaluated negatively they are more likely than fathers' actions to be viewed as irrational. The interpretation of mothers' behavior as irrational links up with the assessment of personality in psychological reports in a way that means mothers' negative actions are viewed as a sign of mental problems, whereas fathers' negative actions are viewed as bad behavior. This does not mean that mothers, in general, are more likely to not be granted residence or custody, because a father whose behavior is viewed as bad is just as likely to not obtain residence with his child as a mother who is deemed to be irrational. This view of mothers' behavior, however, meant that harsher recommendations were made regarding mothers' contact with their children when a mother's actions were viewed as aggressive, obstinate, or unreasonable. Harsh recommendations included limited supervised visitation linked to therapeutic intervention.

EQUALS IN CONFLICT, EQUALS IN COMPROMISE IN SWEDEN

In Sweden the social report writers focused their investigation on the relationship problem between the parents. In other words, the problem of conflict in contested cases was defined as the result of the parents' lack of agreement, but the parents were viewed as normal people. There is a cultural imperative in Sweden, however, for individuals to be agreeable, cooperative, and sensible in conflict in terms of coming to a compromise. The understanding of who is able to compromise is not defined by gendered ideas of who should compromise the most. At the same time, the presence of a dominant parent, as in the cases below, can work together with the professional's attempt to have the parents compromise. This helps to cause an imbalance in which one parent is pressured into compromising, even as it does not resolve the problems that lead to relitigation.

In case SW12 the mother claimed that the father was not present at the birth of the child, and that he would not register as the father of the child without being compelled to have a paternity test by the authorities. However, after the paternity test confirmed he was the father, and before he had met the child, the mother heard that the father wanted joint custody. She did not agree to joint custody, but she agreed that the child and the father should meet. After this meeting the parents agreed on a scheme of contact that would increase over time. Just before they were supposed to meet for a cooperation talk with a social worker, the father, without discussing any of the issues he had with the mother's care, accused her of not caring properly for the child due to the fact that the child had head lice and because father felt mother gave the child too much liquid cereal in a bottle and not enough regular food. Father reported mother to social services. Social services did not find any area of concern and no case was opened regarding the mother's care for the child. When the parents went to the cooperation talks the mother felt under pressure from both the father and the social workers to reach some kind of agreement, and so the mother agreed to joint custody and joint residence. According to the mother, the father was still not satisfied with her willingness to compromise and instead continued to accuse her of not caring properly for the child, which involved trying to get the social services to make a report, which they declined to do for lack of evidence. In a subsequent custody process, the father again went to court, this time to ask for sole custody or sole residence, which the mother would not agree to. While not finding anything remarkable to speak of against the mother's care, the report writers tried to convince her that the father would be the most suitable as resident parent. The social workers wrote their recommendation quoting a few references they found applicable to the case. The first stated that "a mother is the most suitable custodian when a child is small" (as the child in case SW12 was). The second quote, however, claimed that "children do best in the care of the parent of the same gender."[10] In keeping with this schema the report writers recommended that the shared residence continue for the time being, but that father be given sole residence as soon as the child started school. In a rare instance of disagreement, the tingsrätt did not follow the recommendation of the report writers. Instead, the tingsrätt felt that the history of the parents' relationship showed that the mother had the greater ability to compromise and work with the father, whereas the father had been less cooperative and not appreciative of the importance of the mother's relationship with the child. The court ordered that the child be "written in the social register" at the mother's house, but that the visitation schedule be written so that the father continued to have every other week residence with the child. The order meant the arrangement of shared residence for the child would continue, but the father understood that in the future if he returned to court, the court had expressed a preference for maintaining the status quo in the mother's favor.

The presence of violence and aggression in some of the cases introduced a gendered element into what is otherwise a gender-neutral cultural expectation of compromise in Swedish society. The process in the Swedish sample cases occurred further from the point of the parents' relationship breakdown than in the US cases.[11] In other words, the Swedish cases under review in this study were often an outcome of a series of court processes and decisions or prior decisions by the parents, sometimes with the help of a social worker, to reach an agreement. When the cases included tingsrätt or social worker involvement in previous custody decisions, the earlier decision involved an element of pressure to conform to the ideal of compromise, as has been shown in case SW12 above. Pressure was exerted on the parent who was already compromising while the parent who was dominating the situation was assisted in their domination by the focus of the social workers on finding a solution to the disagreement.

In case SW45 conflict was framed by the social workers as a problem occurring in the relationship of the parents, both were seen as equals in terms of their responsibility for the conflict. This was so even though it was clear that one parent's aggression dominated any room left for compromise. The report writers concentrated on the history of the difficulties in the parents' relationship. Current difficulties, however, were evaluated free from any analysis of how the promotion of past custody and visitation arrangements, advocated by social workers or ordered by the court in previous processes, might have contributed to the dominating parent's control of the situation. In her study on Swedish custody cases, Rejmer (2003, 177-184) notes this aspect of the Swedish process, depicting the process as driven toward having couples agree on *something* rather than on a true resolution of difficulties (as this might involve pinpointing one person as more to blame for the trouble than the other). Eriksson (2003, 307-319) confirms how this feature interacts with the presence of violent fathers to produce what Eriksson terms a "non-handling" (in the sense of not managing the conflict or problem) of what are actually domestic violence cases. She states further, "The issue of men's violence has only to a very limited extent been discussed in relation to the (continued) parental cooperation and the well being of children post-divorce/separation" (Eriksson and Hester 2001, 779-799).

In case SW45 the children were removed from residence with their father. The father was accused of physical and mental abuse and a lapse of proper care of the children. They were placed with their mother, who was given temporary sole custody, and the father was given supervised visitation. The children had reported that the father hit them and that he had done this on more than one occasion. Both children gave similar statements, and their report was found credible by social workers. The father was charged with abuse; however, he was not found guilty of abuse. Before the most recent events came the processes that had awarded residential custody of the children to the father in the first place. During the first trial the mother accused the father of abuse and threatening behavior at pick-up and drop-off. From the time of the social workers initial involvement in the custody case, however, the abuse and threatening behavior by the father toward the mother were viewed as conflict between the parents. It was noted in the evaluations as the parents' *samarbetesvårighet* (cooperation difficulty), which was described as arising due to the couple's *inbördes konflikt* (mutual conflict).[12] A conference with the parents was held during one of these earlier processes. The parents stated they were aware that they should not carry out their confrontations in front of the children and instead that they should meet each other in a way which would not negatively affect the children. The mother had been the primary caregiver for the children for most of the children's lives, including while the parents were together, as the father had worked long hours and was often away on business-related trips. During one of the *samarbetessamtal* (cooperation talks) the mother was persuaded to agree to joint residence. The value of reaching a compromise retained the highest priority. Rather than being discouraged from accepting joint residence, given the level of disagreement between the parents, a parent who is looking for a peaceful solution may believe joint residence is the way to pacify the other parent. They may then be supported in that belief by the social worker, as in case SW8:

> [Mother] felt herself pushed into every other week residence at the co-operation talk and felt that her point of view did not mean anything. [Father] decided with the support of the court that [child] should live with them jointly for a trial period. [Mother's statement in the custody evaluation.]

When joint residence was not working for the child, father was given temporary residential custody although the joint arrangement had been in place for only six months and sole residence to father meant separating siblings.[13]

In case SW45 the possible impact that the evident imbalance of power between the parents would have on the future operation of a joint residence arrangement was left unexamined. As in case SW8, once the joint residence arrangement was in place the mother's identification of herself as the primary caregiver of the children was no longer relevant when the parents went back to court. The joint residence arrangement in case SW45 was not successful. At some point during this arrangement the father contacted the authorities and said that mother withheld visitation. Mother contacted the authorities and said that she was worried that the children were suffering due to the parents' conflict. At the same time the mother's move to another area led to the father going to court to ask for sole residence with the children. A custody report was carried out. The custody evaluator in this prior action recommended that the father have residence of the children despite the children's wish to live with their mother. The tingsrätt declared that "both parents could give the children a good and secure environment, but the father continued to live in the familiar home environment." The father's home had not been the children's home for all or even most of their lives. The court stated, however, that "it could not say what the consequences would be of moving the children from their present surroundings." The court also stated that although the children expressed the desire to live with the mother, "the children did not give any specific reasons for wanting to live with mother." A few months after being awarded residence with the children, the father moved with them away from the familiar environment and changed the children's school without notifying the mother. The children later made various claims regarding the father's rough treatment of them:

> The children have suffered from strict discipline from the father and he has threatened to hit them, and pulled their hair, which the father himself has admitted. [The social report writer in the custody evaluation.]

Additionally, the children claimed that he often left them alone for long periods in the evening. The social workers, still constructing equal responsibility between the parents, reprimanded the mother for her lapse in care, saying mother did not protect the children from the inadequate and harsh care of the father:

> The report writer believes that [mother] for a long time has been too passive and has not taken the children's information seriously enough. . . . This seems to be a serious breach of her care of the children [The social report writer's statement in the custody evaluation.][14]

The report writers stressed the parents' equal responsibility for the conflict, despite the fact that the current problem was not conflict between the parents but rather the abusiveness of the father and his lack of proper care for the children. The social workers in the most recent process started to view the father as uncooperative only after he refused to be interviewed for the custody evaluation. In other words, he refused to be listened to. The report recommended sole custody to mother and supervised visitation for the father. The court decided against the recommendations of the social report writer citing, among other things, that although father was charged with abuse of the children he was not convicted of abuse of the children. No conviction of abuse for the father equalized, in the view of the court, the position of the parents relative to the conflict and the tingsrätt viewed both parents as equal in their responsibility for the conflict and in their possibility to stop it. At the end of the process the court exasperatedly stated that:

> The parents should be able to work together. The court finds it ridiculous that two grown people who have taken upon themselves the responsibility to be parents cannot keep the children out of their conflict. [The tingsrätt statement in the final order.]

Joint custody was ordered and father was given a regular schedule of visitation.

The dynamics at play in this chapter impact on the way evidence given by the professionals and experts in both Sweden and the US is interpreted by their courts. The next chapter takes an in-depth look at three cases, and the way in which US and Swedish courts handle professional and expert evidence when there is a problem in the nonresident parent-child relationship.

NOTES

1. Bowermaster's (2002, 265) article discusses the ever-increasing use of psychologists to help judges define best interest in cases where decisions are made about children. Fineman has also expressed her concern about the shift that the concentration on nonlegal sources of decision-making has had on legal decision making involving children. She is alarmed by changes to child custody decisions which have increasingly moved the definition of best interest from a legal basis to one determined by social science professionals and mental health experts. Describing the state of child decision making in the US, Fineman is particularly critical of the increase in extralegal decision making beyond legal scrutiny or appeal (1988, 727-730).

2. Psychologists' reports ordered by the court are considered impartial because the psychologist is not hired solely on behalf of one of the parents.

3. *Breitenfeldt v. Nickles-Breitenfeldt*, 2003 WL 1908070 (Minn. App. April 22, 2003) (unpublished).

4. *McKechnie v. McKechnie*, 1998 WL 15139 (Va. App. January 20, 1998).

5. *Donald v. Donald*, 2003 WL 22515144 (November 6, 2003 Mich. App.) (unpublished) (Levin, J., dissenting) at ¶ IV.

6. *Kirk v. Kirk*, 770 N. E. 2d 304 (Ind. 2002).

7. In Rejmer's (2003, 133) study, in 12 cases in which recommendations by a child psychologist or psychiatrist were included, the recommendation was followed in half of those cases. In the present study there were three Swedish cases where a child

psychiatrist was involved but no recommendations were given as to custody arrangements.

8. *Donald,* WL 22515144 at ¶ IV.

9. In cases decided before 2002, the judge could not order therapy post-judgment.

10. The Swedish custody evaluator was referring to Nissen (1980).

11. See the appendix for a discussion of when the custody dispute processes arise in the parents' relationships; that is whether the process arises in the context of divorce or a longer period after the breakup.

12. Both these phrases, *samarbetesvårighet* and *inbördes konflikt,* are standard in the Swedish custody evaluations when describing the sample case parental relationships.

13. In cases SW6, SW5, SW12, SW35, SW47, and SW34, there were problems with joint residence, but joint residence was nevertheless maintained (in case SW34 the father had problems with alcohol, but the parents came to an agreement after the custody evaluation was written). Joint residence broke down and was not reordered in cases: SW8,SW42,SW45, SW26, SW36, SW19,and SW36. In case SW36 the child did not want to continue joint residence that had earlier been awarded against the will of mother.

14. The mother was the one who brought the accusations to their attention.

FIVE

Cases of Alienation or Problems in the Parents' Relationship?

This chapter closely analyzes and compares cases US19, US21 and SW7, all of which feature problems in the nonresident parent–child relationship. Through close attention to the details of these specific cases, the interaction between the interpretations of justice described in chapter 3 and those of knowledge described in chapter 4 will be illustrated.

PROBLEMS WITH VISITATION IN THE US: A CASE OF ALIENATION

The idea that trouble in the nonresidential parent-child relationship is instigated by an individual, namely the resident parent, led to cases US19 and US21 being refocused from what should have been a decision on the children's best interest, to the US courts viewing the evidence given in the cases according to a schema of whether or not the case could be said to be a case of interference with visitation by the resident parent or not a case of interference with visitation. Understanding why these US cases became refocused in this way must start with a discussion of Parental Alienation Syndrome.

The existence of a set of behaviors exhibited by a child and characterized by an aversion toward one parent and alignment with the other parent was first promoted by Richard Gardner (1987) as Parental Alienation Syndrome. Gardner's thesis of a psychological syndrome known as PAS has become controversial insofar as the syndrome cannot be specifically referenced as the reason, in many US states, for transferring or granting custody.[1] In case US29, for example, the judge distances his reasons for his decision from the idea that his decision might have been based on the discussion of parental alienation presented by the evaluator:

> While [the evaluator] may have relied on the principles underlying this
> theory, this court makes its custodial orders based upon its own find-
> ings of fact, without regard to that theory. [The judge's statement in the
> trial court memorandum.]

Wallace and Koerner's study, however, does give reason to believe that
the alienation concept is still widely accepted and utilized in contested
custody cases. Their study of judicial decision-making criteria shows that
alienation was mentioned by half the judges in the study as a factor to be
given weight, and further that judges still mention *parental alienation* as a
concept, and not merely *alienation* as a factor to be given weight in a
custody decision (2003, 180-188) . Even if judges distance their decisions
from any explicit reliance on Gardner's syndrome, the broader concept of
alienation has been added to the lexicon of US custody evaluators and
expert witnesses. In viewing the events of a case, custody evaluators and
experts may implicitly use an *alienation frame* to describe the actions and
motives of the parents in the case.

Goffman's idea of frames is helpful to understand the interpretations
of the events of cases US19 and US21. Goffman developed the concept of
"framing" to discuss the way in which people make sense of information
and events in the world. A particular schema can be used as the frame
into which all events and information of a case can be organized. Framing
phenomena in this way will have the result that certain information will
be included within the frame and other information left out and take no
further role in the understanding of a situation (1986). A frame, derived
from psychology or quasi-psychology concepts, involves a vocabulary of
suggestive words for describing the people and phenomena of a situation. Once a psychological frame is adhered to it is difficult for the expert
or professional viewing evidence through such a frame to see beyond or
outside the frame, because all evidence gathered from a case can be explained in terms of the frame; the frame becomes self-reinforcing (Bateson 2000, 177-193). Once some aspects fit, all other events and actions can
be viewed as representing a fit, or those aspects which don't fit are left
outside the frame as unimportant. Psychological frames help comple-
ment the view of the professional or expert that the problem is to be
found in an individual, by making sense of an individual's actions and
providing set ways to deal with the individual. Instead of a jumble of
acts, thoughts, and emotions exhibited by the parents and children, the
expert and professional can describe the case as a case of *something*. Such
frames can be used explicitly. Or, as the two sample cases will show, such
frames can also be used implicitly, so that the use of a frame is difficult to
criticize. Once a frame defines the meaning of events, it is used to describe what is viewed as an object which exists in the world (Goffman
1986, 47). Frames such as *alienation* are interpreted by the person using
the frame as an actual and literal occurrence. In the same way that a

medical doctor views a heart murmur, an evaluator observes the interaction of parents and children and describes a case of alienation. The alienation frame produces a set of predictions and solutions that remain strikingly similar to those originally outlined and advocated by Gardner (Warshak 2003, 273-302; Lampel 2003, 232).[2] The alienation frame begins with the observation of what is defined by the evaluator as an *irrational* dislike or stance against a parent by a child. What is classified as an irrational stance by the professional or expert is judged for its irrational quality in terms of the frame; using the alienation frame defines some actions as irrational. For instance, fear, dislike or refusal to visit a parent by a child is viewed as being irrational when the parent, who is the focus of these negative emotions, has been determined by the professionals or experts to be a *fit* parent; that is, the parent is viewed by the professional or expert as an acceptable parent; therefore, the child has no rational reason to be opposed to the parent. PAS was a theory originally conceived as a set of behaviors in children instigated specifically by their mothers against fathers, and although alienation as a concept may be gender-free, some experts are explicit regarding the view that alienation is real and mothers are most indicated in instigating the behavior. Dr. Bob Gordon, for example, a US custody evaluator, stated on his website:

> I agree . . . that most mothers in custody disputes do some form of brain washing. . . . I have done custody evaluations for over 15 years. I have found that mothers' attempts to turn their children against their fathers in custody disputes are very common. I have also found that this is by far the most destructive aspect of divorce on children. I now consider brain washing children against a parent as a form of child abuse, since it leads to enduring psychopathology (Gordon 2008, 42).[3]

The alienation frame may influence a recommendation even when a child is *not* refusing to visit the nonresident parent and is not resistant to having a relationship with the nonresident parent, because the alienation frame views actions that have not happened yet as problematic by imputing to a parent the potential for him or her carry out a plan of alienation. In case US19 the evaluator thought the problems the parents had agreeing on a schedule for visitation pointed to a pattern of alienation attempts by the mother. The mother believed that the father's past misuse of alcohol and what she viewed as his abusiveness were clues to his ability to care properly for their child. The mother's knowledge regarding the father made her concerned (or overly concerned in the definition of the court and evaluator) about overnight visits. The father denied that there were any problems with his care for the child. Instead, he insisted that he would be a better caregiver than the mother; he argued that she was not flexible in terms of her demands for the care of the child and that this inflexibility interfered with his relationship with the child (although the child was not refusing to visit).

The evaluator did not simply depict this conflict over care as misguided on the part of the mother and not in the best interest of the child. Instead the evaluator saw mother's beliefs, motives, and actions as a clue to the mother's attempts to alienate the child from the father:

> In this counselor's opinion, [mother] uses [child's] allergies as yet another means of crafting an alienated father-son relationship. [The family relations counselor's statement in the custody evaluation.]

The professional reinforces the definition of the events as an alienation attempt by using the word *crafting* to define the mother's fears as not genuine, but rather as part of a plan. The evaluator did not view the mother's behavior as just tactical, mean-spirited, or wrong, however, but as evidence of the mother's personality problems. The evaluator quickly dismissed any rational explanations for the mother's preoccupation with the father's care (whether misguided or not). The mother's understanding of the father as someone with an alcohol abuse problem, for example, is mentioned briefly but dismissed unanalyzed:

> [Mother] contends that father excessively consumed alcohol, on a daily basis, during their ten-year relationship. She believes that his problem drinking places [child] at risk when in his care. [Mother's statement paraphrased by the family relations counselor's in the custody evaluation.]

The evaluator did not engage with the mother's claims regarding the father's care, either by clarifying why the mother's fear was not relevant or by completely rebutting the credibility of the mother's claims. The reasons for the relationship breakdown, the father's excessive drinking, were not considered relevant to an evaluation of the mother's claims regarding care. The custody evaluator made oblique references to the father's "passive-aggressive" responses to the mother's demands regarding care of the child, but these unspecified actions of the father were viewed as understandable in light of the mother's behavior. The evaluator did not speculate or analyze how the father's "passive-aggressive" actions might have contributed to a dynamic which helped to continue the conflict. The passive-aggressive actions of the father, for example (understandable or not), might have been seen as fueling the mother's belief that the father was not a trustworthy caregiver. Instead, the mother's claims about the father's care were defined as part of the mother's alienation attempt and could not be considered as arising from any other source. The professional dismissed the mother's fears, characterizing any concerns on the part of the mother as "to be expected" of a mother carrying out a plan of alienation. The mother's actions, which may have been viewed as the mother preparing support for the claims she was making in court, were instead viewed as part of the alienation attempt; what the evaluator described as the mother's "quite predictable and flawed pattern of seek and ally." This "seek and ally pattern" is also described by self-proclaimed PAS experts and advocates. In the excerpt below, for example, Walsh and Bone, writing for a legal audience in the *Florida Bar Law Journal*, claim that one feature of alienation is the alienating parent's ability to get others to support her claims:

> Make no mistake about it, individuals with either PAS or a related malicious syndrome will and do lie! They are convincing witnesses, and their manipulative skills may influence others to follow suit. Furthermore, they have absolutely rational explanations for interference with access and contact by the other parent. (1997, 93-96).

Viewing the actions of parents from a frame of alienation, the evaluator interprets credible evidence given by a parent as too credible. Raitt and Zeedyk's study illustrates a similar circular interpretation of the actions of mothers by experts in English courts in cases designated by those experts as cases of Münchhausen Syndrome by Proxy. Raitt and Zeedyk show how expert witnesses framed, as evidence of mothers' guilt, what might have otherwise been viewed as the normal actions /reactions of mothers in cases involving the sudden death of their infants (2004, 257–278).

The father in case US19 was only asking for a transfer of residence and had not requested that the mother have supervised visitation. The evaluator, however, in addition to recommending a transfer of residence, recommended that the child's relationship with his current primary caregiver be severely curtailed despite the fact that the child had lived with his mother all his life and had expressed the desire to continue living with her.[4] There were no reports against the mother of abuse or neglect of the child, nor any suspicion of mental illness on the part of the mother. On the contrary, evidence pointed to the fact that the mother was a good and caring parent. The evaluator viewed transferring custody and residence of the child as insufficient and advocated for an intrusive course of therapy. The evaluator's frame included a prediction of future action by the mother.

> [This] counselor believes that without therapeutic intervention . . . [mother's] faulty parenting perceptions and behaviors will continue to create emotional and relationship havoc for her son. [The family relations counselor statement in the custody evaluation.]

Even if the mother were no longer the residential parent, the evaluator predicted, "the mother would continue her alienating behavior." The specifics of the "emotional havoc and relationship havoc" that would be caused to the child by the mother's behavior were not outlined. In contrast, the father in the case was viewed as having little role in the conflict. The evaluator did not require any action on the part of the father; he was viewed as the innocent party in the conflict. The mother, being successfully identified by the evaluator as the cause of the conflict, was the only participant in the conflict who needed parent education, counseling and therapy to resolve her personality problems:

> In short, mother needs to engage in counselings and parenting education before she can begin to resolve her personal difficulties that impair her parental role. [The family relations counselor statement in the custody evaluation.]

The judge did not take up the harsh tone of the custody evaluator but noted in a more balanced way that:

> [Mother] is very protective of [child], characterized as overly protective in some ways and I think that is clear. [The judge's statement in the court transcript.] Case US19.

In the opinion of the evaluator, however, visits between mother and child should be supervised and mother should be forced to start a course of counseling before being allowed to have an unsupervised visiting relationship with her child. The evaluator's recommendation was that:

> [T]he father be awarded sole custody of [child]. Mother be granted specific supervised visitation . . . subject to the mother's participation in individual counseling and parenting education. [The statement of the family relations counselor in the custody report.]

The judge agreed with advice regarding a transfer of residence, but declined to make the mother's visits supervised:

> I award joint legal custody to both parents. I am doing that because I believe that both parents love the child, and I don't think the standard is fitness. [Judge's statement in the court transcript.]

The recommendation for supervised visitation and therapy for the mother in case US19 raises the question of whether or not social workers (or lawyers when they have the role of GAL), who are unqualified to make such a judgment, should make recommendations regarding the necessity of a course of therapeutic intervention for one or both of the parents or for the child. Such a recommendation should be made by someone with the proper credentials to judge whether or not therapeutic intervention is necessary. Custody evaluators could suggest that parents or children be evaluated to see if the appropriate expert believes therapeutic intervention should be a necessary aspect of the custody decision. The recommendation of limited supervised visits for mother and child was not followed by the judge, nor was the evaluator's critical tone toward the mother. At the same time, the judge did view the case within the schema of interference with visitation. He noted that:

> It's clear that—well, certainly it's very clear that [mother] for whatever reason and I accept that reason has determined that she no longer cared to be with [father]. Unfortunately, as part of that I think she decided

she needed to protect her son from [father] and the evidence of that is right from the beginning. . . . I think [mother's] conduct has made it difficult for that relationship to develop between [father and child]. [The judge's statement in the court transcript.]

Residence was awarded to the father, who was given final decision making on all questions concerning the child. The judge specifies below:

I should indicate that major decisions with respect to care, education, and the upbringing of [child] should be made by his father and not by his mother. . . . The parties will consult with each other in regards to the child's education, religious training, summer camp, and other activities. In the event that the parties can't agree in those regards, the father will be the decision maker. . . . They have to agree. If they can't agree the father makes the decision. [The judge's statement in the court transcript.]

The inclusion of final decision-making power for the father rendered the final order a sole custody order for practical purposes (however, the mother was given more than the standard visitation schedule). It also signaled the judge's agreement with the evaluator's interpretation of the mother as a person in possession of faulty decision making powers. Despite the order giving the father final decision-making authority, the judge expressed the wish that the father should communicate with the mother in important decisions regarding the child to ensure that mother remained part of the child's life. Later actions by the father depicted him as less than cooperative. The father was, for example, required by court order to return some of the mother's belongings. He complied with this order by using a dump truck to dump the mother's belongings in the middle of a wet road. Contrary to the request by the judge to the father that the father consult with the mother in important decisions for the child, the father refused to include the mother in any decisions made regarding the child. Since the judge's request that the father would cooperate with the mother had merely been an expression of hope on behalf of the court, but had not formed part of the court order, the father was not under any legal obligation to comply.

In case US21 the court process was also oriented toward making a decision regarding whether or not the mother was alienating the child from the father rather than focused on the child's best interests. All the evidence that was gathered in the case was less important in its own right in what it meant for the child than in whether the evidence corroborated or did not corroborate the alienation frame. Specifically, the psychological expert in case US21 used the alienation schema to frame his interpretation of the actions and personalities of the participants in the case. As was shown in chapter 4, there is a gendered aspect to the analysis of behavior interpreted through concepts of mental health. Consequently, the use of a psychological frame to interpret action is more likely to result in an interpretation of negative behavior on the part of a mother as mentally unhealthy or irrational and of a father's negative behavior as bad action.

Psychological evaluations were carried out by the expert in case US21. The results of these tests and interviews were highly critical of the mother, depicting her as involved in an attempt to alienate the child from the father. The psychological evaluator, lifting a description of the mother directly from testing language, described the mother as:

> [A] guarded and defensive woman, who displayed evidence of a mixed personality disorder with histrionic, borderline, obsessive-compulsive, and narcissistic features. [The psychological evaluator's statement in the psychological report noted by the judge.]

In direct contrast, the psychological evaluator described father as "hard working, self-assured, persevering, dependable and trustworthy." Besides these salient features of the father's personality, the judge noted that the psychologist had rendered the following impressions of the father in his report:

> Personality disorder not otherwise specified, with passive-dependent, passive-aggressive features. Father can appear somewhat withdrawn, preoccupied and distracted. [The psychological evaluator's statement in the psychological report noted by the judge.]

However, the psychological evaluator also described the father in sympathetic terms as:

> [A] loving father who wants to remain involved in the child's life. While he may at times show some insensitivity in his comments and jesting with child he does seem capable of exercising good judgment and responsible childcare. [The psychological evaluator's statement in the psychological report noted by the judge.]

Both the mother and child were concerned about the care the child received when with the father. The mother's concerns and the child's wishes regarding the father's actual care were dismissed by the psychological evaluator. Instead, the psychological evaluator set up a narrative of alienation. For example, the evaluator described the father's parenting problems as induced by the mother during the marriage:

> Since father had been . . . disempowered in his parenting role over the many years of the marriage, he will need time alone with child to further the father-[child] bond. [The psychological evaluator's statement in the psychological report noted by the judge.]

Between the first statement in which father is viewed as passive-dependent, and the second in which the father is disempowered as a parent, a picture of a dominating mother starts to emerge. The depiction of the father is of someone made powerless by the mother throughout the years of marriage and this is linked with the idea that it was the father's power-lessness, instigated by the mother, that led to a breakdown in the father-child relationship. The psychological evaluator disregarded what the child said in reference to visits with the father; namely, that the child wanted to spend more time with his father but only if his father took time for them to be alone together. The child's lucid opinion regarding how visits should be carried out were reframed by the psychological evaluator as "resistance to contact."

> It is thus recommended that father have increased time with child de-spite child's resistance to such contact. [The psychological evaluator's statement in the psychological report noted by the judge.]

Having reframed the child's wishes as resistance to contact, the child was viewed as having no rational reason for his stance. According to the psychological evaluator, one proof of the mother's alienation attempt was the mother's false claims of abuse by the father, which gave the impres-sion of mother as a person who was crafting claims in a way that is symptomatic of a case of alienation. Later, however, in the course of the case, the mother's allegations of violence, on the part of the father, were independently substantiated through hospital and doctor's records by the family relations counselor. Even after the abuse claims were substan-tiated the court process proceeded as an investigation of whether or not the mother was engaged in an attempt to alienate the child from the father. Viewed through an alienation frame even substantiated claims of violence can be interpreted as merely a convenient piece of evidence for the alienating parent to use to accomplish the alienation attempt. Once confirmed, the father's violent behavior was not approved of by the court. The fact that the allegations of the mother in this regard could be substantiated, with verifiable outside evidence, was crucial to the judge's perception of the events of the case as not one of alienation, but at the same time, the father's violence was not analyzed as to whether it should be viewed as a potential sign of mental disturbance as such behavior was in the case of violent mothers in the US sample cases. Strikingly, the father *was* manifesting unusual behavior at trial that might have justified a further analysis of his negative behavior. The judge noted:

> [F]ather often laughs inappropriately. The court frequently noted this behavior during [father's] testimony. During his testimony, [father] demonstrated impaired memory, distracted responses to questions, and an alarming inability to focus and answer questions directly. The responses from [father] were so unfocused that the court was com-pelled to ask [father] if he was taking any medication that would im-pair his ability to testify. [The judge's statement in the memorandum of the trial.]

The psychological evaluator had not noted any unusual behavior by the father during his psychological examination:

[H]is reality testing was intact and there was no evidence of cognitive distortions in either the clinical interviews or formal testing. [Psychological evaluator's statement in the psychological report noted by the judge.]

Rather than being a cause for alarm and further inquiry, or a call for therapeutic intervention, the judge seemed perplexed as to what conclusion should be drawn regarding the father's strange behavior. In contrast to the psychological evaluator's report, the family relations counselor concluded that the child had legitimate reasons for acting in the way that he did. That is to say, according to the family relations counselor the child's behavior was not irrational:

[The] child had a factual basis for feeling . . . father was unreliable. . . . [O]n one occasion, Father dropped child off at a swim meet just as it was ending and child had no ride home. . . . On a father/son bike ride, father stopped without telling child and the child suddenly realized his father was not in sight. [The family relations counselor's statement in the custody evaluation cited by the judge.]

The Family Relations Counselor opined that, "the child's comments had a basis in truth though they might be slightly exaggerated." The judge concluded that the mother was not trying to alienate the son from the father, because the son had clearly expressed his wish to continue visiting with the father, but simply wanted time alone with him. Having satisfactorily made his argument against the alienation frame of the psychological evaluator and thus not going against the weight of the idea of a relationship with both parents, the judge gave the greatest weight to continuity of care. Residence was ordered to be with the mother. It was suggested that both parents continue in therapy. The father was not described as having any particular need for intervention despite his behavior although it was suggested that father and child have therapy sessions together.

The frame of alienation used by the professional in case US19, and by the expert in US21, directed the interpretation of the evidence in the cases. At the conclusion of case US19 the judge clearly defined the case as a case of interference with visitation and found the mother to blame for that interference. In case US21 the alienation frame helped to steer the focus of the case so that all the evidence and claims of the parents and the advice of the professional and expert were weighed by the judge against what the claims meant in terms of interference with visitation. The concentration of case US21 on alienation meant other factors in the case, such as violence and the behavior of one of the parents, were left unevaluated in regard to what impact these factors should have on the definition of best interest of the child. It will be shown in chapter 7 that this decision-making focus, although it may leave a primary caregiver with residence of the child, often leaves unexamined the implications that violence has in reference to the cooperation needed in joint custody arrangements.

PROBLEMS WITH VISITATION IN SWEDEN: TROUBLE IN THE PARENTS' RELATIONSHIP

In contrast to the US cases in which individuals are viewed as the root of conflict, in Sweden the relationship difficulty between parents is viewed as the reason for parents' lack of agreement. In case SW7 the child was refusing to go on visits with her father.[5] In common with the fathers in cases US19 and US21, the father claimed that it was a case of interference with visitation instigated by the child's mother. Although this claim by the father was ultimately addressed by the tingsrätt, the professionals did not focus on nor frame the mother as the cause of the problem with visitation, and so the evidence of the case was not used to support the idea of interference with the father-child relationship or to refute the idea. Instead evidence was used to decide whether changing custody or residence would be in the best interest of the child. The report writers looked primarily to the parents' relationship for the answers to the question of why the child did not want to visit with father. The report writers did not dismiss the possibility that one parent might work against the relationship of the other parent and the child. However, concentration on the parents' relationship meant that the context of the past relationship played a larger part in the overall assessment of the case. At the same time, this focus meant that the child's explanation of her refusal to visit was not viewed as a *real* reason for the child's refusal. Instead, the child's refusal to visit with the father was characterized as a mystery by everyone involved with the case despite the child giving clear reasons for her stance.

In one of the few Swedish sample cases where a child psychologist was involved, the psychologist saw the problem as stemming from the unresolved relationship problems between the parents that were unconsciously influencing the child. The psychologist's intervention, however, was not ordered by the court. Instead the mother had sought an explanation for the child's refusal to visit the father. The custody evaluators contacted the psychologist for her opinion about that issue. The psychologist did not give any recommendation regarding what the outcome of the process should be, nor did the psychologist describe the personalities of the parents. Instead, the psychologist felt the mother had translated her own fears of the father's past behavior subconsciously to the child:

> It could never be determined why [child] was refusing to visit with her father. In our judgment it was mother's bitter experience of pappa's care-taking and her fear of leaving the child with him that caused the child's refusal. [The psychologist] said that neither of the parents ac-

cepted this as the answer. The parents did not see that it was unresolved issues between them that caused the child's stance against the
father. [The child psychologist's statement in the custody evaluation.]

Both the mother and father were unwilling to accept the idea that the
source of the child's refusal was linked to their past relationship. The
father saw the problem as connected to the mother's present relationship
with another man and the mother's manipulation of the situation so that
the child did not want to visit with him:

[Mother] has worked against contact and since [mother] met her new
boyfriend nothing in connection to contact has worked. [Father's statement in the custody evaluation.]

In one sense the father was correct. In the past the mother had tried
extraordinary measures to get the father and child's contact to work; even
sleeping on his floor for the first night of visitation on one occasion.
During what was meant to be the father's summer contact he was very
sporadic in following through with contact. The sporadic contact required the mother to take off from work to cover the time that the child
was meant to be with the father. The mother described one of the times
she tried to assist in the contact by calling the father when he did not
show up for contact:

On one occasion [father] was drunk when [mother] contacted him.
When he later came to pick up [child] [the child] would not go with
him. [Mother] after that brought [the child] to [the father's house] and
[the child] stayed there for a few days. [The mother's statement in the
custody evaluation.]

When the contact supervisors could not get the child to go with the
father, the mother offered the father the opportunity to visit with the
child in her home, but he would not accept this arrangement. The mother
became more perplexed by the child's insistence that she did not want to
go with the father, and this made the mother fear that the father must
have done something that "scared the child somehow" during one of his
visits:

[Mother] says that she cannot force the child into contact that she does
not want. [Mother] believes that something must be wrong between
[the child] and [father] for the child to protest so much. [The mother's
statement in the custody evaluation.]

The mother felt justified in her distrust of the father's caring abilities by
her knowledge of the father's drinking and past abusive behavior toward
her:

When she was 3 month pregnant [father] kicked her in the stomach.
She left him then, but they got back together, and he was at the birth.
[The mother's statement in the custody evaluation.]

As the child became more and more opposed to visiting, the mother felt increasingly guilty when she forced the child to go with the father. The child, despite the imputed mystery held by the adults regarding her resistance to contact, gave a lucid account of her reasons for disliking visits with the father. She said the father "had tricked her." He had promised, during one of the visits, if she came with him to let her go home when she wanted to. But when the child asked to go home during this visit, the father refused to let her and instead made the child stay at his house for two more days. The child told the social report writer:

> [I]f pappa wants to see me he has to come to us, I don't want to go to his house, otherwise I won't see him. [The child's statement in the custody evaluation.]

The child also agreed to see the father if someone else came along on the visits. The child felt shy and uncomfortable around the father, as is evidenced by the report of the supervised visitation social workers. She was also uncomfortable in the unfamiliar and very basic living conditions of her father's house, which she described as "boring." Given the child's insecurity in these other areas, and the fact that she could not be in control of the situation at her father's house (she could not go home if she wanted to), it could have been concluded that these factors added to her sense of apprehension each time a new visit was scheduled. The visit she made with the custody report writers in which she was free to decide when she wanted to leave showed that she could feel comfortable with her father if she was able to control the situation. This control needed to stand in for the usual security a child should feel with a parent with whom the child has established trust and faith in the care she will receive. The child had no such trust in the father's care and for concrete reasons not linked to the mother's perceptions of the father's care. The father's visitation was erratic; he did not contact the child or send gifts for the child's birthday or for Christmas. The child and father did not have a close relationship that was breaking down; in contrast, the father was unfamiliar to the child. Furthermore, the father's problems with alcohol were well documented (including an extensive list of alcohol-related arrests). He had arrived for visits on some occasions either not completely sober or shortly after having been drinking. The court itself had concluded earlier that the father could not always follow through on the schedule of pick-up and drop-off because of his alcohol problem. Father continually denied that he had any problem with alcohol, and instead accused the mother of drinking, an accusation for which there was no documentary or other type of proof. Contact persons had been ordered by the court to help smooth the handing-over process.

The underlying focus chosen by the social report writers was that of viewing the problem as one centered upon the relationship between the parents. This meant that the child's behavior remained a mystery, and that the professionals and experts did not really take in as explanatory what the child was saying. There is the expectation that a child should like his/her parent even when there are obvious factors about a parent that should make a child's aversion to a parent understandable. The idea of normal socialization of a child includes within its parameters the idea of unconditional love, not on the part of the parent who is allowed to come and go out of a child's life, but on the part of the child. Sometimes the idea of unconditional love holds true, and children are seen to continue loving, defending and showing loyalty to parents who are clearly deficient in carrying out parental care. In other words, children often love their parents despite their parents' character defects. But this fact may depend on many different features of the child-parent relationship, including the role that a parent has played in a child's life. For example, perhaps children are more likely to be attached to a primary caregiver with character defects, or to a parent with whom they lived for a significant number of years. Despite a child's attachment to an unfit parent in child protection cases, such unconditional love may not be viewed as in the child's best interest to maintain over all other considerations. The point is this, that positive emotions of a child toward parents are viewed as what is normal and best for a child. However, the expectation of natural and unconditional love from a child toward his or her parents reverses the responsibility in the parent-child relationship. Love for parents by their children is not a guarantee. However, it is the taken for granted assumption that children should "like" their parents that arouses confusion in the adults charged with the responsibility of trying to re-establish a relationship between children and estranged parents. Perhaps a different perspective that views a child's love for her parents as not unconditional but as an outgrowth of trust could help to refocus cases in which there is a problem in the relationship between a parent and a child. Also, even though alcohol abuse was an aspect of many of the Swedish cases, as will be shown in chapter 6, there was a hesitancy to implicitly state that a child's negative feelings toward a parent might be linked to the parent's use of alcohol. The connection of inadequate care due to alcohol misuse was easier where older children articulated this connection. The older children's perceptions were accepted as a reasonable attitude to have toward the parent due to the parent's alcohol misuse (as in cases SW14 and SW39). Case SW7 involved a younger child who could not or did not articulate such a connection. The *Länsrätt* (a community court) at which the father pursued the mother regarding her interference with contact had noted that according to the mother's testimony the father's alcohol misuse meant he did not always follow contact agreements regarding pick-up and drop-off. For that reason they had ordered a contact person to be present during pick-up and drop-off. In the custody trial it would have been reasonable for an evaluator to assume that alcohol abuse may also have had a key role in the decline of the relationship between the father and the child. Alcohol misuse caused father to be inconsistent in his contact and increased unfamiliarity between the father and the child. If the social report writers and the child psychologist implicitly understood the connection between the father's problems with alcohol and the child's refusal to visit, they did not state it to be a major factor. The underlying cause of the trouble continued to be viewed as a problem of the relationship between the parents, and particularly the mother's unresolved fears from the past relationship were viewed as a signal to the child that the mother was not happy when the child went to visit the father. According to the evaluators, the planned visit that they went on with the child as part of the evaluation process was positive, and the child seemed to enjoy herself. Before the visit the child had been made promises by the evaluators that they would stay with her during the visit and that she could leave when she wanted to. From this visit they made the following deductions regarding the problems with contact:

> The child's behavior [which was positive as she seemed to enjoy herself] during the visit to her father's house can be interpreted as the obstruction to contact is the mother's signal to the child of her stance against contact, and that the child herself has nothing against contact. It can also be that the trust and security the child felt in us [the evaluator] allowed her to relax and enjoy her visit. [The custody evaluators' statements in the custody evaluation.]

No connection was made in this conclusion, by the evaluators, between the estrangement in the father-child relationship and the sporadic contact that the father had carried out. This aspect of the case formed a separate consideration from the mother's attitude toward contact or the child's increasing refusal to go with the father. Of course, the mother may have signaled apprehension to the child at these times. It seems reasonable to conclude that the mother might have had legitimate concerns regarding visits when the father was drunk and was to collect the child, or when he sent someone else to get the child and she suspected he might be drinking. These concerns need not have had anything to do with the parents' past relationship and could have been concluded as arising within the present context of worrying about the care the child would receive when with the father. The child's difficulties could have been characterized as something more than just shyness and instead might have been viewed as involving a lack of trust that increased every time a visit was scheduled and canceled or scheduled and the father showed up late.

Case SW7 was viewed by the professionals as a case of a problem with visitation, but not as a case of interference with visitation in the way that colored the interpretation of the evidence in the US cases. The report writers viewed the mother's unconscious fears as inhibiting visitation; so on one level the case could be considered a case of interference with visitation. The idea that the cause could be found in the relationship dynamics between the parents, however, rendered the mother's part in the conflict less sinister and did not lead to the conclusion that best interest meant transferring custody. The evaluators defined best interest as the child being able to remain in her familiar surroundings of home, school and friends and with her primary caregiver. In addition to not transferring custody, the evaluators believed that the present difficulties made joint custody impossible, and so they recommended that the sole custody order (to the mother) should stand. When weighing the criteria of continuity (of both care and environment) against the criteria of a relationship with both parents, the tingsrätt did not view transferring custody of the child, in order to ensure the parent-child relationship between the father and child, as in the best interest of the child. In the view of the tingsrätt it was a case of a problem of visitation in which both parents played a role:

> The best for [the child] is that custody should continue to be with [the mother] solely. . . . Contact between [the child] and [the father] has not happened very much and circumstances do not prove that [father] has in any significant or positive way worked to change that. . . . [However] there were no circumstances [shown in the case] that would lead to [father] not being granted visitation. It is instead in the child's best interests that a normal contact can be carried out between [child] and father. If both parents take responsibility to make contact work as the law requires them to do contact can increase as the child gets older. [The tingsrätt statement in the court order]

The father tried to appeal the decision of the tingsrätt in the *hovrätt* (appeals court) but he failed. The hovrätt concluded that the father had not done enough to try to improve the relationship between himself and his child. It was noted that the mother said that the contact between the father and child in the month immediately following the tingsrätt decision:

> Was positive, but since then he has not met with the child [for about a year]. He has not asked to meet his daughter. And [mother] cannot accept him trying to have unscheduled contact with the child. [Mother's statement in the hovrätt decision.]

The idea that the problem of lack of agreement could be found in a problem of relationships framed the investigation in the tingsrätt case. This frame, however, provided a more open assessment of the evidence. There was a greater sense of perplexity regarding what was at the root of the child's refusals to visit with the father, but the evidence was gathered without a sense of accusation against either the father or the mother that was so much a part of cases US19 and US21.

NOTES

1. Connecticut law includes a bar against explicit use of PAS as a reason for rendering a decision. One of the justifications for barring the use of PAS is that Parental Alienation Syndrome is not recognized in the *DSM-IV* (*Diagnostic and Statistical Manual of Mental Disorders of the American Psychiatric Association*). Not all states, however, have specific rules against the explicit use of PAS as grounds for a decision in best interest of the child cases.

2. Stoltz and Ney (2002, 202) provide a more balanced view of the problem, while Bruch (2001) looks critically at both Parental Alienation Syndrome, as outlined by Gardner, and reformed versions of parental alienation which call for less drastic judicial intervention to resolve the problem.

3. Dr. Bob Gordon lists the following accomplishments on his website: Fellow of the APA, past president of the Pennsylvania Psychological Association, twice elected to the governance of the American Psychological Association, Supervisor of the American Association of Marriage and Family Therapists, ABPP and Diplomate in Clinical Psychology since 1982 (2002). www.mmpi-info.com/ (accessed October 4, 2012).

4. Supervised visitation is the recommended action to take in cases of PAS. Rhoades (2002, 71-94) discusses the trend, in the US, of curtailing mother-children relationships in contested custody cases. In case US29 the family relations counselor explicitly referred to Parental Alienation Syndrome in recommendations to the court. The court, while changing residence to the father, concluded that the validity of such a syndrome was not necessary for rendering the judgment.

5. The child in case SW7 was willing to see her father at her mother's house or with some other adult supervising the visits.

SIX

Parents' Narratives of Care

This chapter depicts the ways in which the narratives of the parents, in reference to issues of care, impacted on the process. What type of claims do the parents make regarding their care for their children? What are the parents' reasons for presenting their care for their child in such a way? What issues regarding care do parents raise in cases where sole versus joint custody is being disputed?

PRIMARY CAREGIVER, BETTER CARER, EQUAL CARER

When parents dispute who will be the residential parent they often make claims regarding who was the primary caregiver, who will be the best main carer, or that they are equal carers. Which parents are more likely to make one or the other of these claims depends on their gender and on the society in which the parent is making the claim. In the US cases, continuity of care for children, with the designated primary caregiver, is a criterion to which the court gives special weight. In the majority of the US cases mothers described themselves as the parent with the main responsibility of caring for children in the together relationship, and the US judges most often agreed.[1] As the judge makes clear in the passage below:

> [T]he [father] was involved in the children's lives during the early years on a limited schedule. . . . It is, and should be the undisputed fact that the [mother] was the primary caregiver in the early lives of the children. [The judge's statement in the trial memorandum.] Case US28

Even in the case of a mother who was viewed as very career-oriented, the mother was found by the court to have been the child's primary caregiver:

> Until the parties separation. . . [mother] was . . . primary caretaker.
> When [child] was born [mother] took approximately six weeks off from
> work and then returned to work leaving [child] in the care of a nanny
> during the day . . . during the early years of [child's] life, [mother] was
> intimately involved in [child's] care dressing him in the morning, car-
> ing for him upon her return from work, and arranging his medical
> appointments. [The judge's statement in the trial court memorandum.]
> Case US33[2]

In the Swedish cases, the relationship of mothers and very young children is also a criterion which can be given special weight, but this elevat-
ed status of mother care is considered uniquely important, in contrast to
that of father care, only while a child is very young (particularly nursing
infants). The Swedish courts were less explicit in designating one of the
parents as the primary caregiver. It was clear from the narratives of the
Swedish mothers, however, that they viewed themselves as having a
primary caring relationship with their children, and in addition they
thought this role should play a part in the decision. What mothers in both
Sweden and the US seemed to claim, in addition to the importance of
continuity of care for their children, was legitimacy through a designation of primary caregiver or main carer (in the Swedish case) of the
knowledge they felt they had regarding the needs of their particular
child/children. Mothers stressed that continuity of their care was vital for
their children, and in both the US and Sweden, mothers often made the
claim that the fathers lacked the experience of carrying out the type of
care for the children that the mothers had been supplying. Mothers, who
were asking for residence with the children, claimed that the children
were more accustomed to being in their care (stressing the need for continuity). The mother in case SW8 expresses this thought:

> Mother . . . explains that the [child] has always lived with her, and is
> more bonded to her. During the whole of [child's] life she has had the
> main responsibility for the [child]; because of this she has the insight to
> the [child's] need of closeness and security. [The mother's statement in
> the trial document.]

Similarly, the mother in case US27 differentiates the type of care she
provides from that of the children's father:

> She feels that she has the primary priorities in raising the children
> including taking the children to school, helping them with their home-
> work, preparing dinner, and generally establishing routine in the chil-
> dren's lives. The mother claims that she was the primary caretaker
> while the husband was the "entertainer." [The mother's statement in
> GAL custody evaluation.]

Negative claims regarding father's ability to carry out care could be interpreted in ways a mother did not intend, however. The court or the professional report writers sometimes developed descriptions of mothers as

contemptuous of fathers' ability to carry out care (as in case US19). Such an attitude, on the part of a mother, was equated with the mother not valuing the father-child relationship. Although it may be true that the other parent did not have the experience of carrying out care to the extent the primary caregiver did, the ability to carry out proper child care by the nonprimary caregiver was taken for granted by the evaluators in both countries. Primary caring mothers had to navigate a paradoxical situation; in the real world, mothers in the cases had been carrying out the care of their children along fairly gendered lines; in the court process, meanwhile, mothers needed to promote their experience of caring for their children and stress the importance of this continuity of care for their children, and yet they also needed to unlink the narrative from a too explicit idea of this care as gendered or as a belittling of the importance of the fathers' role.

Fathers, on the other hand, in the US cases, did not try to dispute the mothers' claims that mothers had been the primary caregiver for the children in the past. Instead, US fathers in cases for residential custody made the claim that they would be *better* carers regardless of who was the primary caregiver in the past. The father makes this idea clear in the case below:

> Father feels sure he will do a better job raising his daughter. He makes sure there is structure in the home. [Child] is always in bed by 9:00 pm. . . . He likes to teach [child] educational skills. [The father's statement in the GAL custody evaluation.] Case US36

In this same case the mother expressed the concern that the father was not really carrying out care when the father had the child with him, but was dependent upon the grandmother to carry out care of the child. The mother in case US36 raises an interesting point regarding whether fathers are more likely to request custody if they have a partner or female relative who can help with child care, and whether or not judges are more likely to award custody to fathers if there is either a new female partner or other female relative in the paternal home. Two studies have shown, at least in the US, a larger percentage of single-parent fathers are in live-in relationships when compared with single-parent mothers (Fields 2002,10; Casper and Bianchi 2002, 131).[3] A related study of self-reporting adult children also shows that child care-taking tasks are likely to be gendered when a father remarries, even when he is the nonresident parent; step-mothers tend to be the individual taking primary responsibility for the children during visits (Schmeeckle 2007, 174-189).

In Sweden, less emphasis was placed on the designation of a primary caregiver in the evaluations and in the court decisions, although mothers reported taking maternity leave after the birth of the children, whereas the fathers did not report whether they took paternity leave. In keeping with a narrative of equality as sameness, Swedish fathers pointed to the fact that their relationship with their children should be viewed the same way it is viewed for mothers.

> [T]he [child] needs her pappa the same as her [mamma]. [The father's statement in the custody evaluation.] Case SW6

The court and evaluators held the perception and expectation that Swedish fathers could and should be equally involved carers. Also, a larger number of the Swedish cases took place a longer period after the breakdown of the parental relationship when compared with the US cases. Most mothers in the Swedish cases had been the primary caregiver when their children were infants, but there were more Swedish cases in which the father currently had residence with the children or where the children lived jointly.[4] Joint residence arrangements in Sweden meant that whoever might have been the primary caregiver before the joint residence arrangement was put in place was no longer viewed as the primary caregiver once the joint arrangement was in place even if the arrangement was new and of short duration. Swedish mothers sometimes expressed the criticism that they had been pressured into agreeing to a joint residence arrangement, and when shared residential agreements broke down, after a relatively short period of time, mothers did not view the primary caregiving relationship, between themselves and their children, to be significantly changed from what it had been prior to the shared residence arrangement; they did not view themselves as suddenly not the primary caregiver. One mother (US45) described a situation in which she was still carrying out the majority of care-taking tasks despite the joint residential arrangement; for example, the children would only be bathed and have their hair combed during the week at their mother's house.

HOW THE CHILD IS DOING

A key question in the formulation of what is in a child's best interest, and related to the designation of a primary caregiver, is "how is the child doing in the present residential arrangement?" The answer to this question impacts on the parents' claims regarding care in different ways in the US cases when compared with the Swedish cases. How a child was thriving in the current arrangement was an important question for the court in both the US and Sweden. But the question "how is the child doing in the current situation?" was most likely to impact on the assessment of care being provided by the primary caregiver in the US cases. If the child was viewed as doing well, the judge often linked this factor to the efforts of the primary caregiver. In this case continuity of care was given the most weight provided that the nonresident parent and child were having regular visitation, as the excerpt below depicts:

[C]ounsel for the minor child reports that [child] now presents herself as a "great, well adjusted and flexible child." . . . "She is a resilient child who does not require a lot of discipline or limit setting . . . [and who] evidenced a tolerance for disappointment and imperfection even at her young age. . ." The court notes the significance of the fact that [child] has developed these salutary personality and developmental characteristics while she has been residing with her mother, subject to her mother's scheduling and social protocols, and visiting with her father on a regular, anticipated and periodic basis. [The judge paraphrasing the attorney for the minor child's statements in the trial memorandum] Case US10

In case US10 the professional was advocating for a change in the residential plan; however, the child's positive characteristics were attributed to the care given by her residential parent.

The most successful narrative, on the other hand, for a nonresident parent to develop in the US cases when requesting residence or a transfer of custody was to focus on how the child was doing when the child was not doing well, as in case US13, where the father was asking for a transfer of custody:

He [father] also became convinced that the [mother's] parenting style was having overall negative consequences for the child in virtually every aspect of [child's] life and was not confined simply to outburst surrounding visitation . . . the [father] believes that the [mother] will not or cannot follow through on providing stability for the boy and in getting professional help for [child] needs. [Father's testimony paraphrased in the trial court minutes.]

Just as a primary caregiver can claim responsibility when a child is doing well and stress the desirability of maintaining the child's current custody situation, a primary caregiver can also be held responsible if the child is not doing well while under the care of the primary caregiver. There is a difference between the Swedish and US view in this context. In Sweden, because the concentration of both the professionals and the court was on the relationship problem between the parents, the relationship problem between the parents was viewed as a possible source of stress and anxiety for the child, and so provided an alternative explanation why a child might not be doing well in his/her current situation. This being the case, the idea of "how the child is doing" did not always impact negatively on the assessment of the primary caregiver's care when the child was not doing well in the current arrangement.

TROUBLE AGREEING ON CARE

Not all contested cases involve issues of residence.[5] In cases where parents already agreed on where their children would live contested issues arose regarding whether the custody type would be sole or joint. In these types of cases two issues involving care were often raised by the parent wanting sole custody: the issues of medical care and problems with substance abuse. Agreeing on medical care was more of an issue in the US cases, whereas the presence of alcohol and/or substance abuse was more of an issue in the Swedish cases. In both societies there is the subtle idea that asking for sole custody does not show a cooperative spirit on the part of the parent asking for sole custody. A parent asking for sole custody might be framed as merely possessive and controlling. He or she may be depicted as not satisfied (almost in the sense of being greedy) with the fact of having residence of the children, and this points to the possibility that such a parent is merely working to exclude the nonresident parent from the life of his or her children. In both the US and Sweden, however, joint legal custody or shared parental responsibility sets up a legal requirement that residential parents and nonresidential parents communicate regarding all major decisions involving their children. The sample cases show that contrary to the idea of greedy and possessive residential parents, sometimes joint parenting becomes fraught with difficulty. In case US57, for example, the father rendered joint decision making impossible by refusing any communication with the mother, including receiving information regarding the children's visits to the doctor:

> Father refuses communication in any form with his wife. He refuses or hangs up on her telephone calls, returns her letters unopened, and rips up her notes in front of her. The only way the mother can communicate with father, about the children and the visitation schedule, is through their attorneys. [The judge's statement in the trial court memorandum.]

Similarly, in case SW44 the mother could not discuss anything with the father without him becoming extremely angry:

> Mother does not see any possibility of contacting the father regarding the children. The child [the older verbal child] according to the mother also does not want her to talk to the father because [as the child says] "he gets so angry then." [The mother's statement in the custody evaluation.]

During pick-up and drop-off this same father would not respond to the mother in any way, pretending not to hear any comments she made and saying nothing himself.

A major feature required by parents in joint custody arrangements is cooperation on issues of care involving nonemergency medical treatment. In the US, in particular, problems arose with the care of children when parents disagreed regarding children's medical diagnosis and the administration of doctor-prescribed medication for that diagnosis. An example of where this issue arose in the US is when a child had been diagnosed with Attention Deficit Hyperactivity Disorder (ADHD), or a related disorder for which medication was prescribed by a doctor.[6] In the cases where a child was diagnosed with ADHD the mother had typically sought medical treatment for the child after the child had displayed significant behavioral problems. Conflicts over medical intervention for a child often led to the court process itself. In case US16, for example, the father refused to administer the children's prescribed medicine. The resident parent wanted to have sole custody as a way of compelling the other parent to follow the doctor's recommendations. The judge concluded that the father in US16 was capable of deciding whether or not the children should be medicated:

> [Father] is capable of assessing whether [the children] are in need of stimulant or ancillary medication during his time with them but only if he participates in the children's treatment processes. [The judge's statement in the trial court memorandum.]

In case US16, however, the relationship between the parents had deteriorated so much that the parents had to meet for visitation exchanges at the local police station. Additionally, the judge's statement in case US16 regarding father's participation in the children's medical care was not part of the order made and so was not legally binding on the father (although it may have been a warning regarding the outcome of a future court process on the same issue). The court had, nevertheless, specified that the father could decide whether or not to give the children their medication. The father was not legally compelled to participate in the children's treatment. By failing to confront the obvious lack of cooperation in the parents' relationship, cooperation which is needed in joint decision making, the judge had legitimated the father's refusal to administer and provide consistency for the children in their medical routine when they were under his care, a potentially devastating inconsistency in care. The only way the court could have insured that the father follow the children's medical treatment would have been to give mother sole custody or, as is allowed in the case of Connecticut, mother could have been given final decision-making power when it came to decisions regarding medical treatment. Unless a judge is willing to suspend a parent's scheduled visitation, however, when the parent does not follow a particular course of medical treatment there is no way to ensure that a parent complies with his or her child's course of medical treatment. Since the criterion of having a relationship with both parents is given great weight in the US the court is unlikely to invoke punitive actions such as limiting visitation or ordering supervised visiting to force compliance with nonemergency medical treatment. In case US38 the father also refused to give the child the prescribed medication:

> [A]ccording to the testimony, the father objected to the regimen of medication that the child was on and withheld it from the child. [The judge's statement in trial memorandum.]

In another case (US34), the father refused to give the child medication while the child was in his care. The professional in the case speculated that the inconsistency in administering the child's prescribed medication may have played a part in the tragic accident in which the child was killed. Due to the nature of the accident it was suggested that the child's lack of medication at the time of the accident may have contributed to the circumstances of the child's death. The quote below was from a custody evaluation made before the death of the child:

> [T]his case surrounded the parties' inability to agree that [child] needed . . . medication to combat . . . [anger control management ADHD disorder]. The mother consistently administered the medication. The father held a consistent opinion that the medication affected [child] too severely and that [child] did not need his medication. [The GAL's statement in the custody evaluation.]

In a statement from the child to the GAL, the child admitted that although he liked not taking his medication, he also recognized that he became "wild and got into trouble" when he didn't. The mother in case US34 was requesting sole custody of the children. The father's violence and problems with substance abuse were also factors in the mother's request for sole custody. The court ordered shared parental responsibility of the remaining child. The case is discussed further below and in chapter 7.

In case US30, which also involved aggression on the part of the father, the father opposed medication for the children who had been diagnosed with behavioral problems. This refusal involved threatening the child's pediatrician. The court noted:

> [Father] believes that children's problems would vanish if the children did not consume so much sugar. [The judge's statement in the trial court minutes.]

In another case (US5), conflict arose between the parents regarding the child's asthma and the doctor's recommendations regarding the child's treatment. The court had additional concerns regarding the father's care of the child, as shown below:

> [T]he father wrote a confrontational letter to child's pediatrician that caused her to lose the services of the doctor she had had since birth. He was also careless in his actions with respect to child's asthma. He continued to smoke cigarettes in the house and he refused to provide her with appropriate medication. He failed to keep his handguns in a locked storage area. They were kept in an open bowling bag under his desk, easily accessible to his child. [The judge paraphrasing the custody evaluation report.][7]

The issue of proper administering of medication and conflict over medical diagnoses did not enter into the case narratives in Sweden. The difference between the two countries regarding the issue of medical care can be explained by the link that medical advice has with proper child care in the Swedish context when compared with the US. In Sweden doctors are considered experts in the administration of proper care. Everyone has access to medical care. The idea of universal medical access renders the care of doctors something which everyone expects to receive as a member of Swedish society—especially children, for whom such care is free. In other words, medical care is viewed as a necessity and a human right and not as a commodity. In the US, although doctors may be held in high regard, medical advice is viewed as something that is variable; one can shop around for different medical opinions. Medical advice and medical care is a commodity, and this view impacts on the assessment of parents who hold contrary views to doctors' advice regarding their children. In Sweden a parent might hold alternative views to a doctor's advice regarding medical care and treatment for their child, but such a stance toward the advice of a doctor would have to be carefully explained to the custody evaluator or the court. Doctors are viewed as experts in proper care; a parent deciding in an ad hoc way to go against a doctor's well-considered advice for a child would be viewed in a highly critical way by both the custody evaluators and the court and would probably impact on the assessment of that parent's ability to cooperate with the other parent in caring for the child.[8]

ALCOHOL AND SUBSTANCE ABUSE

Alcohol and substance abuse was a significant issue in the Swedish cases—but featured less in the US cases. Twenty out of the 53 Swedish cases involved parents with alcohol or drug problems. Mothers had problems with alcohol abuse in 4 out of the 53 Swedish cases. Fathers had alcohol or drug problems in 13 out of the 53 Swedish cases. In 3 additional cases both parents abused alcohol, but in these cases the mothers' substance abuse was greater in severity (cases SW10, SW14 and SW49). The incidence of substance abuse noted in the Swedish cases is in agreement with a key point of Rejmer's study of Swedish custody cases. Rejmer found that as a group the parents in her study were overrepresented in the area of alcohol and drug abuse (2003, 72-77). Although unsubstantiated allegations of alcohol or drug use could be one possible interpretation for the accusations of one parent against the other, in the Swedish cases that involved alcohol abuse, other evidence besides the report of the accusing parent substantiated the allegations. Evidence that pointed to truth of the claims included police reports of drunken disorderliness, or the propensity for a parent to have many convictions for drunk driving. The problems with substance abuse impacted on abusing parents' ability to care for their children and had led to a custody conflict. Substance abuse was an important factor in protective parents' reasons for wanting sole custody. The father in the case below describes how the alcohol problems of the mother impacted on the care the child was receiving when the child was in the mother's care:

> [Father] saw that the child was not doing well. He saw that she was not properly cared for. She was dirty. Also, the child told him that she had to eat alone. Later the parents agreed that the child would move to father's.... [The child] was according to him very unhappy, had a hard time sleeping at night, cried a lot and asked a lot of questions about death. [Father] thought [child] needed the calm and security of settling in [his town], but because of joint custody he could not decide himself on the change of school. That is when he turned to the court to try and get sole custody. [Father] wants sole custody, he does not have confidence in mother, he wants to be able to stop visits [with mother] in the case that [child] is in jeopardy at mother's house. The child at those times is restless and speaks nervously. [The father's statement in the custody evaluation.] Case SW9

The mother in the case above did not think her problems with alcohol made her an unsuitable custodian. In her opinion, agreeing to let father have residence was proof she was cooperative and so she and the father should share custody of the child:

> [Mother] wants to keep the joint custody arrangement that they have had from the beginning. It is important that she has a part in decision making both for herself and for [child]. She also thinks it feels more secure with joint custody in the case that something happens to father. [Mother's statement in the custody evaluation.]

The Swedish court agreed with the mother regarding the parents' ability to cooperate. The court reasoned that since the parents could cooperate there should be no worry about the child's care as the child was already living with the father. Despite such reasoning by the court, not having sole custody often meant that a protective parent could not take the immediate action they needed to when the other parent's substance abuse problems began to escalate. In case SW9 there were already some indications that the situation for the child at the mother's home was deteriorating. The court stated that the father did not need to have sole custody, because he could return to court if the situation at the mother's home became unacceptable; however, this seemed to be exactly the point the father was making, but it was a point which the court was not willing to act on.

Case SW43 demonstrates the difficulty with joint custody as a custody arrangement in cases where one parent is both a substance abuser and violent. In SW43, the mother had been the child's main caregiver in the together relationship and she stressed that the child was most accustomed to her care. Alcohol abuse on the part of the father had led to the breakup of the parents' relationship. Mother was also subjected to abuse from her ex-partner and described the father as dominating her. The father's alcohol misuse impacted upon the mother's idea of proper care of the child. In other words, she had a firm basis for viewing the joint custody arrangement as not in the child's best interest. She had been attacked and threatened by the father during pick-up and drop-off times. When the parents separated they had joint custody with the mother as the resident parent. After a summer visit, however, the father refused to return the child to the mother. The joint custody arrangement meant that the police could not forcibly take the child from the father because he was a legal custodian of the child. To make matters worse, the mother could not contact father or the child during this period, because she would have broken the *no contact order* in place against the father. The father would not allow the child to call her. The child expressed his wish to live with the mother to the custody evaluator, but he was afraid to tell his father. Eventually the child was returned to his mother. At the point of the present proceeding, the mother wanted to change the joint custody arrangement to a sole custody arrangement:

> [Mother] wants sole custody of [the child] because [father] broke the agreement that they had regarding summer visitation. . . . [Mother] did not get to contact [child] for the whole summer. The police could not help her they said because they [parents] had joint custody. . . . [Mother] did not know what was happening with [child] but she knew that [father's] drinking had increased. . . . [The child] on several occasions during that summer was left home alone while father went out. . . . Because of the threats he [father] made against her, the assault, and the breaking of the protective order [father] was sentenced to three months in jail. . . .[Father] has used the child's telephone to leave threatening messages for mother. [The mother's statement in the custody evaluation.] Case SW43

What made a difference in the outcome of case SW43, and led to the order of sole custody for the mother, was not the circumstance of retaining the child during summer vacation or even the father's lack of proper care of the child and abuse of alcohol. The factor which tipped the balance against joint custody was the conviction of the father for assault and threatening.

In case SW30 the father had a problem with alcohol and was abusive in the parents' together relationship. He assaulted the mother while she was pregnant with their second child.[9] After the couple separated they agreed on a joint residence arrangement for the children; however, the father refused to let one of the children return to the mother's residence during the period the children were scheduled to live with her. He also made false allegations against the mother in order to back up his actions. Nevertheless, after withholding the child, he was given temporary custody of the child he withheld. Later, in the continued dispute processes, due to the weight given to continuity of environment, father was given sole residence of the child he had withheld but not residence of the child's other sibling. The court agreeing to this arrangement resulted in the separation of the siblings. During the period of time that father was the resident parent, father abused alcohol, including during times when the child was present. The father was subsequently arrested for violence to his new partner. After the father's arrest, the mother was given temporary residence of the child. In the most recent process, the mother was seeking sole custody of the child. Sole custody was granted due to the father's incarceration for assaulting his current partner. As in case SW30 above, Swedish mothers sometimes regretted accepting a joint residence arrangement when the father's problems with alcohol or abusive behavior made such an arrangement difficult:

> Mother never wanted joint residence but was afraid to go against the father's wishes (he was threatening and abusive). She feels that the father is not suitable as a custodian. The child and father should have a lot of contact as the child loves her father and he is a good father when he is sober. . . . The child is overly quiet has bad self-confidence and her drawing shows that she is not doing well. [Mother's statements in the custody evaluation.] Case SW6

The court, however, refused to end the joint residence arrangement, viewing it as the child's stable arrangement.

Compared with the high number of Swedish cases in which substance abuse was an issue, there were only seven US cases raising verifiable claims regarding alcohol or drug abuse.[10] It might be that obvious cases of alcohol abuse were more likely to be resolved prior to a contested process in the US, or that problems with alcohol were not a feature of what instigated custody processes in the US. The issue of alcohol or drug abuse when it arose was viewed seriously by the US judges:

> [Mother] testified credibly that [father] periodically drank to excess and that she frequently argued with him about his abuse of alcohol. [The judge's statement in the trial court memorandum.] Case US33

In the US cases, alcohol abuse mitigated the idea of continuity of care in cases where the primary caregiver parent had a significant problem, as in case US20 (this was the only case where a primary caregiver mother had an alcohol dependency problem). Despite the serious stance the court took in cases US20 and US33, making an allegation of alcohol misuse might be viewed as more of a problem than the misuse of alcohol. In case US19, for example, which was analyzed in chapter 5, the mother was convinced that father's alcohol use impacted on the care he gave the child. A parent may have firsthand experience of the drinking behavior of the other parent, which makes the protective parent concerned regarding the care the child receives while with the substance-using parent,

especially when a child is very young; but US judges and custody evaluators make a distinction between a substance abuser, whose problems can
be verified, and a parent who is not strictly speaking an alcoholic but
who allegedly does not provide good care to his or her child when drinking, the difference being the latter case is much harder for a protective
parent to prove as it is more likely to be viewed critically by the judge
and custody evaluator as either a false allegation or as overembellish-
ment of the other parent's normal alcohol use. In case US17 the court was
not convinced the mother was actually concerned about the father's alcoholism, viewing the mother's raising of the issue as tactical:

> The court is skeptical, however, of mother's testimony that the father
> sometimes has alcohol on his breath when he takes the children for his
> parenting time. In view of the conflicted nature of this dissolution case,
> the court suspects that she would, if such had actually been the case,
> have notified the family relations counselor, police or the family court
> that her husband was driving with the children while intoxicated. [The
> judge's statement in the trial memorandum.]

There seemed to be an indeterminacy in case US17 as to whether the
father's drinking was a real concern of the mother, or simply the mother's
overplaying the issue for the sake of the court. The mother's concerns
were not viewed by the court as totally fabricated, however:

> [Father] attended a substance abuse program and Alcoholics Anony-
> mous because the incident that led to his arrest and a protective order
> had involved his use of alcohol. The evidence is mixed about whether
> that problem has continued since the parties finally separated. Al-
> though the [father] admitted that he no longer attends Alcoholics
> Anonymous and drinks at home on the weekends, both parties told the
> family relations counselor several times that alcohol abuse was no
> longer an issue. On the other hand, the [mother] testified at trial that
> following the [father's] return home after the protective order his
> drinking problem became worse. She sometimes smells alcohol on his
> breath when they exchange custody of the children. [The judge's state-
> ment in the trial court memorandum.]

Despite the judge's skepticism regarding the mother's motive in making
the claim, the judge ordered the father to undergo a substance abuse
evaluation:

> Nonetheless, her concerns raise such a significant issue affecting the
> potential safety of the children that the court's orders will require the
> father to undergo substance abuse evaluation and any treatment rec-
> ommended. [The judge's statement in the trial court memorandum.]

In case US34, discussed earlier regarding medical treatment for one of the
children, the father had a problem with both drugs and alcohol. Even
though the problem of substance abuse was fairly well established, the
social report seemed to question whether the mother was merely using

the evidence to score points as opposed to analyzing the mother's real fear of the father's care due to this problem. This hesitation to understand allegations as something more than attempts to get the upperhand in the US cases is crucially important if and when any future action on the part of the protective parent becomes necessary. If allegations are not taken with enough seriousness before a protective parent takes an action, such as withholding visitation, then such an action may be judged harshly as interference with the other parent's relationship with the child.

The gender-neutral forum of the court process means that gendered terms and connotation for child care must be discarded. At the same time, mothers wanted and felt the need to stress their historic role as primary caregiver for their children. Since this was the case for both US and Swedish mothers (and Swedish mothers did not have much to gain by making a case for that role), it can be viewed as a need beyond simply trying to have an advantage in the process. US fathers in the cases often declined to dispute mothers' claims to be primary carer. Instead, US fathers claimed they would be better carers. Such a stance can be effective in the US cases when a child is not doing well, as the child's present condition may reflect upon the care a child is receiving in the present situation, as has been demonstrated in previous chapters. Swedish fathers were more likely to answer mothers' claim of being the main care giver by noting that children need their fathers in the same way they need their mothers. Two features impacting on care played different roles in the US as compared to Swedish cases. Conflict over medical treatment appeared in many US cases and led to mothers asking for sole custody even when they already had residence with the children. In the Swedish cases problems stemming from alcohol and substance abuse led to protective parents claiming they needed to have sole custody to protect and properly care for their children.

NOTES

1. In eight of the US cases a designation of a primary caregiver was not made. In case US8 the father was the primary caregiver.

2. Maume and Mullin's (1993, 533-546) study shows that a majority of men are resistant to being responsible for child care while women work and when the men are, women are likely to either stop working or women try to find alternative modes of daycare. This finding suggests one reason why women are likely to be primary caregivers for their children, especially in the US where child care may be difficult to arrange.

3. Fields's (2002, 10) analysis of US census data shows that single fathers are more likely to be in a co-habiting relationship. In around 33 percent of single-father homes the father is co-habiting.

4. For further information on the characteristics of the cases, see the appendix.

5. See table 3 in the appendix.

6. In cases US11, US16, US24, US30, US32, US34, US38 and also US24 the fathers had problems dealing with the children appropriately due to the children's behavioral

problems. In case US5 the parents had trouble agreeing on what doctors the child would have.

7. The professional in this case recommended joint shared residential custody. The court disagreed.

8. However, a recent inclusion in Swedish law allows for children to receive care against the will of one of the parents in a joint custody arrangement if a social worker finds the services to be in the best interests of the child.

9. Use of alcohol tended to be combined with abusive behavior on the part of fathers in the Swedish cases. One Swedish mother with alcohol problems was also abusive and threatening (SW20).

10. Accusations of alcohol abuse in cases US12, US37 and US8 were considered far-fetched by the court.

SEVEN

Violence and Abuse in the Parents' Relationship

A recurring narrative in the sample cases was a claim by one of the parents that the other parent was physically and verbally abusive. This chapter looks at the issue of intimate partner violence raised in both the US and Swedish cases. What impact did abused parents think aggression and abuse should have on the definition of best interest of the child? How was physical confrontation between parents interpreted by the court and professionals?

GENDER AND INTIMATE PARTNER VIOLENCE

In both the US and Swedish cases, fathers were more likely to be the perpetrators of violence, aggression and verbal abuse. Violence and abuse by fathers against mothers in the sample cases was evident already in the pre-breakup relationships and continued to be an issue after the parents' separation. Other studies have found a link between contested custody cases and the level of violence between the parents in the pre-breakup relationship (Jaffe and Geffner 1998; Johnson 2005, 284-294; Keilitz 1997; Kurz 1995, 158). Violence, verbal abuse and/or stalking was part of the narrative describing the parents' relationship in more than half of the US cases.[1] In a majority of US sample cases, where violence was an issue, a father was found by the court to be an aggressor against a mother.[2] In three US cases judges clearly viewed mothers to be the aggressors against fathers; however, mother on father violence had a different dynamic which will be described further below. In eight cases, mothers alleged violence and abuse on the part of fathers and while the court did not consider the allegations false, the court did not draw any conclusions

101

regarding the allegations.[3] These cases are not included in my total of father on mother violence above. The point is to give rigorous support to the finding of the gendered nature of violence in the contested cases by using the US judges' own interpretations of who the aggressor was in the majority of cases where violence was part of the narrative.[4] In the eight cases where physical conflict was viewed as mutual by the judge, violence was irrelevant to the decision at least in terms of viewing the cases as needing to be assessed as a "domestic violence case."[5] The judicial attitude seemed to be that violent interaction between the parents was more symbolic of a couple's overall inability to get along than an area of concern for the safety of one of the parents. Viewing violence as mutual impacted on the assessment of the dynamics of aggression in cases such as US50. In US50 there were credible witnesses who testified to the aggressiveness of the father against the mother in their together relationship, but during one incident the mother was arrested along with the father. Dual arrest framed the conflict as mutual. Such a situation points to the difficulty with laws and policies put in place to protect domestic violence victims by mandating arrests or allowing warrantless arrest during domestic violence incidents.[6] Police arrive at a domestic violence scene, for instance, where each participant involved in the altercation blames the other and both are arrested. The impact of dual arrest on the assessment of domestic violence in the custody process was more of an issue for mothers than fathers as none of the cases in which mothers were clearly the aggressors were framed as mutual. When domestic violence is framed as mutual some of the typical characteristics of an abused person's demeanor were interpreted negatively for mothers for the reasons outlined in chapters 4 and 5. When a mother exhibits defensive, negative behavior, for example, against the father this can be interpreted by psychological experts as indicating a personality problem or by the judge as not being a "friendly parent." A parent may be described as guarded and defensive, for instance. When a parent's extreme action, due to fear of their partner, results in dual arrest the dual arrest acts as a leveler of responsibility for the violent dynamics at play in the relationship. In case US57, for instance, there were multiple incidents in which the father's violence had prompted the mother to call for police intervention. An expert on intimate partner violence might interpret the mother's actions, firing the gun at the floor to warn the attacker, in case US57 as arising from fear of the father's impending abuse; however, in the custody dispute neither parent was determined to be the primary aggressor, because both parents were arrested during the incident, the father for battery and the mother for illegal discharge of a firearm. The judge below describes the event that led up to the arrest of the couple:

> After the party, mother accused the father of drinking too much, resulting in a physical altercation during which mother hit her head. At some

point during this altercation, mother pulled a .38 pistol out of the night-stand and shot into the floor of the apartment. Father was charged with spousal battery and mother was charged with illegal discharge of a firearm. The couple attended several counseling sessions to satisfy the criminal court and the charges were dropped. [The judge's statement in the trial court memorandum.]

Assault in the incident is re-imaged by the language which describes the abuse as if it were self-inflicted. For example, the mother is described as "hitting her head." In the context of a custody trial hard evidence, such as arrests records, builds a particular story of the case. Just as an arrest and conviction for domestic violence may turn a case into a conclusive domestic violence case, cases in which both parents are arrested can result in a narrative of mutual confrontation. The main aggressor is likely to use this narrative to his advantage by insisting on the narrative of mutual aggression. In such a he said she said situation a judge tries to reflect on which parent seems the most credible, or a judge may not make a firm finding regarding who is the main aggressor because the judge can come to a decision which incorporates the understanding that one parent might be the aggressor without having to specify one. For example, a judge can make an order for residence of the children with one parent rather than the parent the judge thinks is more aggressive. This state of affairs, however, will most likely mean that an abused parent will have to interact with the abusive parent in a shared or joint custody arrangement. The idea that accusations of violence, even those considered true, are often used tactically strengthens the likelihood of an interpretation of mutual aggression. A judge, perceiving both parents as unreasonable, by virtue of their engagement in the custody conflict, may hesitate to give one parent an advantage in the process by declaring one parent more at fault for the aggressive interaction than the other.

Despite the ideal of equality between men and women in Swedish society which might suggest fewer attempts at physical domination of men over women, violence by fathers against mothers was also a feature in the Swedish cases. In 19 out of 53 sample cases, fathers engaged in violence and threatening behavior against mothers.[7] In the Swedish cases, as in the US cases, violence by fathers against mothers was evident already in the intact relationships and continued in the post-separation relationships. The case below provides an example:

Mother said: [father] has a hot temper, soon after they moved in together, he revealed that he had uncontrollable moods when he hit her with a closed fist. [The mother's statement in the custody evaluation.] Case SW38

In both the US and Sweden, violent conflict in contested custody disputes cannot be viewed as arising from the contentiousness of the custody process itself, a common way of framing violent behavior in custody processes. In their study on violence, Tjaden and Thoennes have also found that most victimization begins in the intact relationship (with the exception of stalking which is more likely to occur after separation) (2000). In contested custody processes, the level of abuse and aggressive interaction in an intact relationship may give rise to the custody conflict, rather than the other way around. This dynamic was not evident in mother on father violence which (with the exception of case SW20) took place after the breakup of the parents' relationship, and in some cases was the reason the fathers were asking for residence of the children (US29 and US37).

In contested custody cases there is the idea that allegations of violence are often false. In US society the perception that allegations are false has enough legitimacy to impact policy. Florida law, for instance, makes specific reference to "the making of false allegations" in custody disputes in the statutes governing the decision-making process.[8] Even when the fact that violence has been a dynamic in the parents' relationship is not disputed, raising the issue of violence may still be viewed as merely a tactical, overembellished narrative. For this reason, violence may play an ambiguous role even when the allegations are accepted by the court as not being fabricated. Legal criteria which specify that domestic violence may be given weight in a custody decision, or statutes which contain a rebuttable presumption of child residence with the abused parent, are dependent for the strength of enforcement on the court viewing violence as a particular kind of violence. A judge, for example, may regard the descriptions of violence as true and still may not view the case as "a domestic violence case."[9] The US judges in the sample cases were aware of issues surrounding intimate partner violence and the issues that it raised in custody and visitation decisions.[10] One judge stated, for example:

> An order of joint custody requiring parties to consult and make decisions jointly would be highly problematic if a history of abuse created such an imbalance. [The judge's statement in the trial court memorandum.] Case US53

On the other hand, what rises to a level of violence that creates "an imbalance" is interpreted through the discretion of individual judges in the US, and the narrative the judge develops regarding the actions and motives of parents in a particular case. Linking the conflict to a problem of individuals, US judges tended to look negatively on an accusing parent if they viewed that parent as merely trying to gain leverage from the fact that the other parent had been violent on a few occasions. In some cases, judges found the allegations totally untrue. Claims of violence that were considered false by the court were extremely damaging to the accusing parent's character assessment, as in case US12, discussed in chapter 3. The seriousness with which judges view false claims of violence calls into question the idea that a mother need only mention the specter of intimate partner violence to be awarded custody and withhold visitation from the father. Even in the US cases where violence was considered present, however, and not a fabrication, custody evaluators and judges sometimes, either explicitly or implicitly, viewed the raising of the issue as a tactic used by the mother to gain an advantage in the process. It is correct to specify mother in this instance because no accusations by fathers, in the US cases, were framed as using what were considered "true" allegations tactically. In case US3, for example, the mother claimed physical abuse as the reason for the breakdown of the marriage:

> [Mother] perceived the [father] as a violent, aggressive and angry man claiming physical abuse at the hands of the [father] on five separate occasions. In addition to the physical abuse, [father] would repeatedly belittle her, calling her stupid on repeated occasions. The [father] denied all claims of physical abuse and did, however, admit that the parties engaged in verbal combat in the past. [The judge's statement in the trial memorandum.]

The GAL in the case recommended that residence be awarded to the father. The judge in the case found the mother's allegations credible. This fact, however, played a small role in the decision which was based on the fact that the mother had been the primary caregiver.

> The court . . . does not accept the father's contention as approved by the guardian ad litem that father is the better custodial parent. . . . All of the witnesses presented by the mother . . . testified that the mother was and is a good mother. She was characterized as loving and attentive in the upbringing and rearing of her children. [The judge in trial court memorandum.]

Experts and professionals in the US cases tended to recommend against mother residence more often than the judges, even in cases where a father was violent. The judge, however, did not link the father's aggressive behavior toward the mother with a reduced ability to care for his children:

> The witnesses also testified that the father loved his children. They further confirmed that while the children are in his care and custody he is also attentive and loving. [The judge's statement in the trial court memorandum.] Case US3

Earlier chapters have made clear that a link is made, in the US cases, between mothers who are aggressive to fathers and aggressive mothers' care for children. No such automatic link or assessment was made for fathers who were aggressive and threatening toward mothers despite the body of research which confirms the link between spouse abuse and child abuse (Edleson 1999; Hambya and Finkelhor et al. 2010; Ross 1996; Rumm et al 2000;)

In the Swedish cases if an abusive parent was not just charged but also convicted of abuse, domestic violence was assessed as a factor in the decision. As the court reiterated in case SW51:

> The court makes the following consideration: according to the decision of another court, [father] on some occasions committed serious offenses and assault against [mother]. [The court's statement in the summing up and order.]

And in case SW17:

> [Father] was charged in December for assault and threatening behavior against [Mother] and given a suspended sentence. Again he was charged in March for threatening behavior in front of [children] in which he threatened to kill their mother. He was sentenced to four months in prison on the grounds that he was at risk of continuing his illegal harassment.

The court concluded, in case SW17, that the father was not committed to changing his behavior and this fact made joint custody unworkable.

> [Father] is committed to violence and threatening behavior against his former partner. He does not accept the sentence that was leveled against him. It is inevitable that [mother's] experience of this should influence her future relationship with [father] and her ability to work with him in questions regarding the children. [The court's statement in the summing up and order.]

In both cases the Swedish court ordered sole custody for the abused parent:

> The tingsrätt agrees with [mother's] opinion that it is best for the children if she continues to have sole custody and that they live with her. [The court's statement in the court order.] Case SW51

And in case SW17

> The court finds that [mother] has presented good reasons to be against joint custody. With support from the custody report, the court finds that it is in the children's best interests that there is no change in custody and that [mother] continues to have sole custody of [children]. [The court's statement in the court order.]

In cases where the violent partner was not convicted of violence the factor was considered more ambiguously. One Swedish study has shown, however, that even in cases where a parent had been convicted of a violent crime against a family member many violent parents were still awarded joint custody of children (Barnombudsmannen 2005, 2).[11] In the Swedish sample cases, where a violent parent had not been convicted, the court viewed the fact that residency could be specified as a sufficient measure to protect the abused parent. In this view, sole custody was only considered necessary in the most flagrant abuse cases where the severity of the abuse was proven by a conviction for violence. The lower Swedish courts were supported in this view by the higher courts, which tended to look less on whether violence was an issue and more at whether the parents seemed to be able to agree on at least some decisions regarding the children. This deduction, by the court, was made by referencing the issues that the parents had agreed on.[12] A violent parent may have agreed to the residence arrangements, but not to the residential parent having sole custody, for example. In agreeing to the residence arrangement a violent parent had shown himself to be cooperative and reasonable. In this instance, the abused parent's perception of an unequal power relationship and domination by a violent partner, as the mothers in the Swedish sample often interpreted fathers' aggressiveness, was not sufficient to have the court award sole custody.[13] The court in case SW15 made this view clear when the judge opined:

> According to the court such a fear does not weigh more than [child's] right to have contact with both parents.[The court's statement in the summing up and order.]

In the above case the court refers to the mother's fear not weighing more than the child's right to contact with both parents. The description by the court seemed to frame the situation as one of no contact by father versus contact for the father, with no contact being based on the mother's unfounded fear of the father's violence. A closer look at the case shows that lack of contact between the father and child was not the issue. The father in case SW15 had regular visits with the child. The mother was not against this contact nor was she interfering with it. The trouble arose when the father wanted to increase the amount of contact he already had to include weekday visits and to be awarded joint custody. The mother felt that sole custody had worked well enough and that father wanted more contact with the child as a way of continuing the aggressive behavior he displayed at pick-up and drop-off times during which he sometimes threatened to strike her:

> The father tries to start fights with her when he picks up the [child] that is why she makes him pick up the child at the door to the building instead of her flat. [Mother] says [father] still when he does not get his way raises his hand to her. [Mother's statement in the custody evaluation.]

The father in case SW15 carried out other types of abusive behavior, such as spitting in the mother's face. The court and the professionals did not view these incidents as untruthful. But the mother was framed by the professional and court narrative as if she was merely being uncooperative in reference to the reasonable request for more parenting time from the reasonable father. On the other hand the mother was, from her point of view, trying to reduce the number of times per week she would have to come into contact with the father and his abusive behavior. The influence of the father's own aggressive acts on the child's impression of the father during pick-up and drop-off interactions was not viewed as significant, but the allegation that the mother told the child that the father hit her in the together relationship was. What the mother viewed as not submitting to the father's domination, the court and the professionals viewed as the mother's equal responsibility for the father's aggression. In fact, the mother was viewed as mainly responsible for negatively influencing the child's impression of the father, while the father's own aggressive and threatening behavior in front of the child was not seen to have any significance on the child's well-being. The mother's concerns about the father's continued attempts to dominate her actions and decision making for the child through the imposition of joint decision making that is required in joint custody were described by the report writer as the mother's attempt to "shut the father out of his child's life," rather than the report writer assessing and trying to find solutions as to how the mother could avoid the father's aggressiveness if the report writer's recommendations were followed. Additionally, the father was not required to take responsibility for his own actions and, more than that, was confirmed in his thinking that such actions were appropriate behavior. The court process had allowed the father a forum to continue the control he exercised over his former partner.[14]

A mother's personality and attitude could also be used as a gauge of her safety from an abusive partner. Such a dynamic was evident in both the US and Sweden. In case SW6 the mother wanted to discontinue the shared residency arrangement, because the father continued to be aggressive, but the mother was described by the custody evaluators as having "a strong personality" and this feature of her characterization was seen as evidence that the mother was able to deal with the father's aggressive behavior. Furthermore, the mother's strong personality was viewed as indicating that the mother was not in any real danger from the father's violence. Despite the continued violent interactions between the pair, the residential arrangement was viewed by the court to be successful:

> The shared residential custody has for the most part worked well except that the parents' relationship since the separation has not been good. [The court's statement in the summary and order.]

Since the couple were in court due to the fact that the interactions between the parents were highly confrontational, it is left to conjecture what part of the arrangement was working well. Perhaps the court was referring specifically to whether the children were cared for properly when in each parent's care? Research, however, has pointed to a correlation between the negative impact of parents' continuing conflict on children's well-being (Amato and Rezac 1994; McIntosh 2009; Mechanic and Hansell 1989; Whiteside and Becker 2000). Given that shared residence arrangements have become more common in recent years, further research is needed to learn about the effect of continuing parental conflict (especially conflict involving aggression and violence) on children who live in shared residence arrangements.[15]

Similar to the Swedish cases, judges in the US cases could interpret an abused parent's actions as a gauge of an abused parent's safety. This is a feature which points to a misunderstanding of risk in situations of intimate partner violence. An abused parent's risk for further abuse should be determined by reflecting on the level of violence, or the persistence of violence and threats of the perpetrator, rather than on the victim's personality, demeanor or behavior. Campbell et al. (2003) point out various factors which increase the risk of homicide in cases of domestic violence. These include factors such as whether the abusive partner has a gun or has threatened to kill the abused partner or threatened suicide. An assessment of a victim's risk should not rely solely on the victim's behavior and still less on the victim's personality. In case US53 the father was violent, as narrated by the judge:

> The mother claims the father was repeatedly physically and verbally abusive to her during the marriage. She testified at the trial here that there were approximately 50 physical altercations between the parties during the marriage. She said that the father would lose his temper, throw things at her, push or shove her, and call her derogatory names. She testified at trial that at least twice he punched holes in walls or broke objects. She also claimed that the physical and verbal abuse continued after they separated. [The judge's summary of the mother's testimony in the trial.]

The judge noted, however, that the father claimed the mother instigated his violence:

> The father acknowledged at trial that there had been physical disputes between the parties during the marriage but asserted that the mother was always the instigator and his own actions were only defensive in nature. [The judge's summary of the father's testimony in the trial memorandum.]

The judge in the case found the mother's version of the father's violence in the marriage to be truthful. It was the mother's actions, however, that were important to the assessment of what weight the violence would have in the decision:

> The evidence also shows that the mother has a tendency to provoke or bait the father, to which the defendant has in the past overreacted. [The judge's statement in the trial memorandum.]

The father was depicted as lacking control, but this lack of control did not reflect on his character assessment in terms of raising any concerns regarding his mental health. Instead father's behavior was directly related by the judge to the mother's actions and demeanor. In other words, in this case, acting violently was within a range of reasonable, if inappropriate, actions that a person might take when provoked. What "provocation" may be considered as understandable in its ability to incite someone to violence is not discussed. The judge remarked, for example:

> On numerous occasions he [father] has been unable to resist the mother's provocations and reacted inappropriately. [The judge's statement in the trial memorandum.]

The mother's actions were used by the judge to determine that the father posed no real threat to the mother, because as the judge described it the mother's actions proved that she was not afraid of the father. Here again, as in the Swedish cases, the assessment of the mother's safety was based on the mother's actions rather than those of the person responsible for the violent behavior. For example, the judge opines:

> Despite abuse inflicted on mother in the past, the evidence clearly shows that she is fully able to function as an equal to father in interactions regarding their children. She stands up to him, challenges him, baits and antagonizes him, and sometimes even dominates him. [The judge's statement in the trial memorandum.]

In effect the judge is saying that the mother can stand up to the father. She instigates the abusive behavior. Although the father's behavior is not condoned, there is no analysis of whether the father poses a danger to the mother or the children outside of viewing the mother's actions and reactions to the father's violence, despite the fact that the psychological report on the father in this case was not positive and revealed some areas that should have signaled a cause for concern. The case is particularly illustrative of the way in which an abused partner's attitude can be used to determine the level of danger the abusive partner poses to them. If the abused partner does not react as a victim within a judge's understanding of what a victim should act like, then the significance of the abusive acts on the outcome of the case and the assessment of safety of the abused parent are imperiled.

If not showing enough fear can impact on the assessment of what role violence will have in a US decision, showing too much fear may also impact negatively on an abused parent's case. Calling the police often for an abusive parent's breach of a no protection order can be depicted as a disingenuous attempt to gain leverage in the custody contest, even in cases where there is documented abuse. In the case below the father's violence was not in dispute, and he was also known to abuse drugs. But through the use of the phrase "each and every time" the GAL seemed to point to the excessiveness of the mother's actions and to put in doubt whether the mother was reacting out of genuine fear of the father. Similarly, the guardian's phrase "even been suspected of" frames the mother's response to the father's actions as extreme. In fact, the words "each and every time" in the guardian's custody evaluation were underlined by the judge as if these words gave a clue to the mother's intention to use the allegations for a strategic purpose:

> The mother has made serious allegations against the father, which include domestic violence and stalking. The mother has informed the authorities *each and every time* [emphasis added] the father has even been suspected of violating the outstanding domestic violence injunction or his probation. [The GAL's statement in the custody evaluation.] Case US34

If a person subjected to intimate partner violence turns to a support group she is likely to find just such advice as that which the mother in the case above seemed to be utilizing. One information site, the Marie De Santis Women's Justice Center, for example, contains the following advice:

> Immediately report each and every violation of the restraining order. This is so important to women's safety. But many women don't do it, often because they feel very embarrassed to report minor violations. (2007)

In case US34 the father had a history of disregarding court orders as well as requests made to him by the GAL. It was not unreasonable for the mother to believe that he might also disregard the protection order. If a mother reacts with too much fear of her abusive partner, the mother is at risk of being perceived as merely using what is accepted as a substantiated claim of violence in an opportunistic way. This state of affairs leaves abused parents in a catch-22 situation. It is reasonable for them to try and protect themselves. It is also reasonable of them to think that the violence of their partner might be taken into account in a custody decision where the couple will be required to work at joint parenting, or where the residential placement of the children is at stake. However, if raising the issue of substantiated abuse by the other parent is to be put under suspicion it begs the question of whether abused parents in the US are placing themselves in a worse situation by bringing up the allegations, or whether they are better advised to downplay the fact of abuse in order to be perceived as the "most friendly parent."

PARTNER ABUSE AND CARE

While court and professionals often viewed violence as a separate issue from care of a child, an abused parent often made a connection between a parent's abusiveness and the abusive parent's care for the child. Parents in both the Swedish and US cases who were subject to abuse described how violence and threatening behavior impacted upon their ability to insist that the other parent take proper care of the child or children. In case US34 as outlined above the father had a history of assaults on the mother. The fact that the mother was fearful of the father meant that she had no way of compelling him to care properly for the children. For example, she claimed:

> There were several allegations from mother that the father was expos-
> ing the minor children to adult situations . . . including but not limited
> to excessive drinking while boating, adult nudity and adult videos.
> [Child] admitted that he had witnessed those things and the father
> agreed . . . to stop taking the children to [place]. [GAL's statements in
> the custody evaluation report.]

But subsequent events showed that the father did not always keep his word to the GAL.

In case US30 the mother's difficulty in controlling and disciplining the children was instigated by the father who (as shown in chapter 4) was also aggressive and threatening toward the mother:

> [The father] admitted to totally sabotaging the children's schooling in
> order to visit vengeance upon the children's mother. [Father's state-
> ment in the custody evaluation.]

Even when inadequate care was not carried out as a purposeful action to punish the other parent, the abused or threatened parent had limited means by which to compel an abusive parent to carry out proper care; for example, in cases SW45 and SW43 the children were often left alone while the fathers went out at night. The children in these two cases were too young to be left alone and were fearful, but both mothers lacked the ability to compel the fathers to carry out care more responsibly, and as was shown in chapter 4, when returning to court in order to compel proper care by one parent the issue was framed in the Swedish cases as a problem in the relationship between the parents. That is, the concentra-tion was placed on the parents' inability to agree rather than on address-ing the issue of care or abuse.

Due to the father's violence against the mother in case US21 (dis-cussed in depth in chapter 5), the mother tried to avoid meeting at pick-up and drop-off times. Attempting to avoid meeting up with the father, however, meant the child was left alone when the father failed to meet the child at the arranged time and place for contact. On numerous occa-sions the mother or other carers for the child received calls from the frightened child because the father had not shown up to collect him:

> [Father] was late in picking [child] up at the [place] on more than one
> occasion. The child made tearful telephone calls to the other adults in
> his life because he was upset and frightened that his father failed to
> pick him up at the scheduled time and place. [The judge's statement in
> the trial court memorandum.]

This same father exposed the child to dangerous situations while the child was in his care, one of which led to injury of the child. Another area where violence and domination was claimed by one parent to impact on care was when children were witnesses to violence or threats against the abused parent, as in the case below:

> [Father] abused her and [child] was a witness to that. . . . [Father] threatened to kill [mother]; the [children] were afraid and unhappy of what might happen to her. [The mother's statement in the custody evaluation.] Case SW17

In some cases, children were frightened not just for the abused parent but for themselves as well, as in case US37:

> The children were also intimidated and fearful of her flaring behavior. [The judge's statement in the trial court memorandum.]

Fathers who had been the victims of aggressive or threatening behavior were just as likely as threatened mothers to describe the violence of the other parent as impacting on the child:

> It is not good for [child] that mother comes to his flat and screams and fights that affects the child badly. [The father's statement in the custody evaluation.] Case SW20

Despite the parents' linking the violent behavior of an abusive parent and the violent parent's care for the child, in both the Swedish and the US cases, that link was not analyzed sufficiently by experts and professionals. A large body of research is available regarding the negative impact on children from witnessing or exposure to violence perpetrated by one parent against the other (Bogat et al. 2006; Fergusson; Graham-Bermann and Seng 2005; Hester 2007; Holt, Buckley and Whelan 2008; Perry 2005; Whitfield et al. 2003). In case US30, the GAL recommended that residence be awarded to the father, despite the father's aggressive threats and action toward the mother and the father's sabotage of the children's schooling as a way of punishing the mother. The judge in case US30 did not agree with the GAL's recommendation and instead significantly reduced the father's visitation. In Sweden only a conviction for violence against a parent led to an assessment of the violent parent's care for the children. There was a gendered interpretation of the significance of aggression when care and aggression were linked; the aggressive behavior of mothers toward their former partners was linked with the mothers' care for their children. Violent mothers lost or were not awarded residential or joint custody, and violent mothers were given supervised visitation. None of these violent mothers were accused of physically abusing their children, but in case US37 the children were afraid of the mother and there were cogent reasons for ensuring the children did not have any contact with the mother's boyfriend. The mother in the case lost residence and received supervised visitation.

In both the US and Sweden the pre-breakup relationships of the couples often involved abuse prior to the custody process, with the exception that violence on the part of mothers often began after the breakup. Fathers were more likely, in both the US and Sweden, to be perpetrators. At the same time, when entering the court process, violence and abuse often became framed as mutual conflict, and even when violence was not framed as mutual, an abused parent's attitude, behavior, and personality may be more determinative of how the abuse was interpreted by professionals, experts and the court. Finally, abused parents linked the abuse they suffered at the hands of their ex-partners to the care the other parent was carrying out for the children, because the abused parent lacked the means to compel an abusive partner to care for the children in a responsible and dependable manner. Asking for sole custody, or returning to court to change a joint custody to a sole custody order, is one of the means by which abused parents hope to ensure proper care for their children. In the context of Sweden the problem of care, viewed as a problem in the parents' relationship, may not be properly addressed. In the US, if an abused parent's narrative of abuse is framed as tactical and viewed as being used to gain an advantage in a custody dispute that parent may not be viewed as the most friendly parent, a characterization that can be detrimental to the protective parent's demands for custody type or residence with the children.

NOTES

1. Thirty-five of the US cases included issues of violence and abuse of one parent against another. In three of these cases the mother was the clear aggressor (US23, US29, US37).

2. In seventeen US cases judges viewed fathers as the main aggressor. By strict interpretation I refer to the fact that I relied on the judge's interpretation of an event or relationship as a violent one and did not merely include a case in this total if one participant made an allegation of violence. Cases with allegations which were regarded as false by the court (such as case US12) are excluded from this total.

3. Cases US7, US10, US13, US31, US50, US61, US66, and US54.

4. However, it would be incorrect to add the further eight cases in which mothers claimed violence against them to the total of mutual violence or even more incorrectly mother on father violence.

5. At least ten states have a rebuttable presumption that joint custody of children with a partner found to be the perpetrator of domestic violence is not in the best interest of the child. Thirty-four states have domestic violence as a factor which can be considered. A further 17 specify a rebuttable presumption against joint custody for a parent who is batterer.

6. Twenty-three states have mandatory arrest laws (National Justice Institute 2008). However, individual state and state jurisdictions set their own policy regarding whether or not to have officers assess a primary aggressor in the situations. The NJI report found that the percentage of male victims being arrested with their female

perpetrator was higher than for females being arrested with male perpetrators; however, that particular dynamic did not impact on the cases in this study.

7. Mother on father violence had a different dynamic in that mother aggression arose in the context of the custody or visitation disputes and was not a feature of the together relationship, with the exception of SW20. Additionally, these mothers were aggressive and threatening, but there were no instances of them battering fathers.

8. Florida Title 6 Chapter 61.13(3)(k). Evidence that any party has knowingly provided false information to the court regarding a domestic violence proceeding pursuant to s.741.30.

9. Levine and Mills (2003) have looked at outcomes of cases in states where rebuttal presumptions govern cases in which violence is a factor and states where violence is one factor which can be considered, and have found drawbacks to each of these schemes.

10. There is a great body of literature tailored to the needs of judges regarding the issues involved in intimate partner abuse and domestic violence; for example, Keilitz 1998; Dalton 2006; and Robert 2002, to name a few.

11. In the Barnombudsmannen study on contested custody cases it was found that in 18 out of 42 cases, where a parent had been convicted of a violent crime against a family member that parent was awarded joint custody of the child (2005, 2). Swedish law has subsequently made it easier for courts to decide against joint custody in more contested cases by taking away the presumption of joint custody. See Regeringens proposition 2005/06:99 and NJA 2007 s.382

12. The Swedish Riksdag has expressed the opinion that "joint custody against the will of one of the parents should be precluded if the other parent is subjecting a member of the family to violence, harassment or other abusive treatment." Ministry of Justice Fact Sheet, *Custody, Residence, and Contact* (1998).

13. A half a year after separation 95 percent of previously married parents have joint custody. For parents who previously lived together but were not married the figure is 84 percent (Schiratzki 2002, 90).

14. The social report writer thought the father should have an increased visitation schedule, referring to Sjösten's book that suggests a more innovative approach to visitation schedules (1998, 88).

15. For example, 20 percent of children in Sweden whose parents do not live together live in joint residence (Statistiska centralbyrån 2004, 13). In Wisconsin, Melli and Brown (2008) found that shared residence parenting increased from 2 percent to 32 percent during the 20-year period to 2001. Some US states have a presumption of shared residence when parents can't agree on custody arrangements, for example, Louisiana Rev. State. §9:335, Art. 132; while Idaho has a statutory presumption of shared residence: Idaho Code §32-717B(4).

EIGHT

Children's Opinions in the US and Sweden

This chapter looks at the place of children's opinions in the process. In what ways do children's opinions impact the definition of best interest in contested cases in Sweden compared with the US? What is the underlying basis in the US and Sweden for giving children an opportunity to voice an opinion regarding the process they are caught up in?

THE RIGHT TO A VOICE AS STATUS CONFIRMING OR ACTION SORTING

In Sweden the law concerning the inclusion of children's opinion in situations where a decision is being made about them can be viewed as status conferring (Honneth 1992, 92-139). That is, the right to be heard is used to confirm the status of a person who is entitled to expect certain considerations. One of these considerations is the right to contribute to, or voice an opinion regarding, decisions that will impact on one's life. The right to be heard is an inherent part of being a person (a human right) and as such involves a moral obligation on the part of other morally acting adult persons to offer the opportunity to children to be listened to. This moral obligation means that the opinions of children be actively sought, even the opinions of young children (Barnombudsmannen 2005, 6). Case SW22, for example, demonstrates the Swedish evaluator's attempt to actively engage with the children in the case (eleven and eight years old) to discover if they have anything to say regarding the situation:

> After a while we begin to draw their family map on a big paper on the wall. We draw the children in the center and mamma and pappa on top. Then we draw in their grandparents. When the family map is

finished we begin to talk about the divorce again and if they have any
friends who have separated parents. They do but they don't talk about
the separation with them. They have a little difficultly talking about
their parents' separation and we wonder how they would have things
if they could decide. They are a little unsure and don't answer. [The
social report writer's statements in the custody evaluation.][1]

The impetus for the inclusion of the right of children to have a voice in
decisions made about them in Sweden arises from the discussion of "the
rights of children" as it is found in the United Nations Convention on the
Rights of the Child (UNCRC).[2]

In contrast, following the ideas of Honneth (1992, 92-139), laws pertaining to children in the US can be viewed as action sorting. US laws
regarding children, including the inclusion of the criteria to consider children's opinions in best interest cases, sort actions into what is acceptable
and unacceptable behavior toward children. Children are viewed as
needing protection from the actions of adults due to their status as dependent and innocent, rather than their deriving status due to a moral
understanding of children as people who have human rights. Laws pertaining to children in the US, including the inclusion of the opinion of the
child criterion, are a matter of action sorting. Child protection laws vary
from state to state; for instance, the amount of physical punishment
which is considered acceptable varies.[3] In contrast, in Sweden the law
against physical punishment of children is not solely to protect children
against overly harsh punishment, but is also regarded as a matter of a
child's right not to have to endure physical punishment for any reason (it
is a human right not to be violated by physical pain inflicted by another
person, whatever the proposed purpose of the punishment).

One difference in focus between the US and Sweden, regarding the
opinions of children in contested cases, is observable in the use of children's opinions as evidence in US cases rather than as a way of understanding children's ideas regarding how they want the situation being
decided to work out. In the US the question can be asked in any given
case, is a child's opinion being considered or is it being used as evidence
against following their wishes? Children's opinions can be used as a
piece of evidence not just by the judge, but as a piece of psychological
evidence by the professionals or experts who are charged with making
recommendations in a case. A child's opinion becomes psychological evidence once it is viewed as needing analysis to discover something about
the child giving the opinion rather than the opinion being used as a way
of finding out what a child thinks about the current situation or what she
hopes will happen after the decision is made. It is an important distinction to clarify which role a child's opinion and voice is occupying in any
given case. Is a child's opportunity to voice an opinion fulfilling an obligation to the child as a matter of right? Or is the child's opinion being
analyzed as a piece of psychological evidence? Viewing the child's opin-

ion as psychological evidence does not mean that a child's wishes will be disregarded by the adults in the case, who may or may not judge that the child's desires are not in the child's interests, but that a child's opinion can be used for evidence without considering the child's wishes. Whenever a process moves from the idea of finding out what children think about a situation as a matter of their right to voice an opinion, to that of one criterion among others that are guaranteed by law in the collection of information about a case, there is the danger of moving toward an analysis of children's opinions rather than the *regarding* of children's opinions. Regarding what a person says implies considering what a person says to be a legitimate desire for someone to have voiced. This is not the same as saying that the listener will judge that the speaker is making a good choice for themselves, and consequently taking into consideration other aspects of the case the expert or professional might recommend, which may be something contrary to the wishes of a child. Some utterances may be a cause for alarm, as for example, when a child expresses the opinion that she wishes she were dead. But what about in a case where a child expresses a strong dislike for one of her parents? Perhaps a child says something along the lines of, "I don't want to live with my mother because she is a dirty pig." Should such a statement be regarded or analyzed? An argument can be made for or against analyzing what a child says depending on the circumstances of a child's life, but analysis of what someone says should not be confused with the right of that person to express an opinion. To be analyzed, to have one's opinions analyzed, and to lack any choice over whether one is analyzed should not be confused with the right to have one's opinion heard and considered.

MATURE CHILDREN'S OPINIONS

In many jurisdictions in the US the law provides for considering the child's opinion based on the maturity of the child giving the opinion. Maturity is judged, for the most part, on the age of the child. The justification for tying age and a greater ability for children to impact the decision is that older children can communicate their wishes more effectively and understand the consequences of their own choices. Another consideration of older children's opinions has less to do with respect and allowing children a voice, and more to do with the fear that older children can take action if they are forced into a situation against their will. Older children can run away. The issue of being given a voice out of a moral understanding of respect for a child as a person versus that of a child's opinion having the ability to be weighed with other evidence ties in with the tension in the US between the fear that older children will take action if they are forced into a situation against their will, and the idea that older children should do as they are told. If older children refuse to follow the court's decision they can be viewed as out of control, and this perception of mature children can itself impact on the definition of best interests. When issues of control arise, older children's opinions in the US can become a focus of analysis, and a case meant to decide on issues of custody or visitation can spiral into an effort to control the actions of children rather than providing opportunities for children to voice their opinions and to have the reasons they have for holding those opinions considered.

Case US67, for example, involved a long series of court processes over a period of years in which the father, through the efforts of his parents, tried to have visits with the child against the wishes of the mother and child.[4] The child clearly expressed her desire not to be forced to visit with either her father or his parents. Pick-up and drop-off times during visits were filled with confrontation. The first psychological evaluator declared the mother unfit, due to what he viewed as the mother's negligent failure in forcing the child to follow the court-ordered visits. The question of the mother's fitness did not arise in any other area of the family's life outside the psychological evaluation context. Later, when an update of the psychological evaluations was required by the court, the child refused to speak to this same evaluator who, the child claimed, "thought she was stupid." The court concentrated on the issue of control in relation to how the mother was teaching the child to obey court orders, rather than focusing on the child's reasons for refusing to speak with the psychological investigator, and despite the fact that mother stated that "the only way she could get [child] to cooperate with [psychologist] would have been to physically force her."

According to teachers in the child's school, the child was happy, well adjusted, and doing well. She had won various prizes for her talent as an artist. There was no basis, outside of the court process, for defining the child as problematic. The analysis of the opinion of the child as something that could be used to demonstrate the state of the child's mental health seemed only to manifest itself within the psychological interviews with the first psychologist and was not supported by any observations of the child in her everyday life (apart from refusing visits with her grandparents). In an interview with a subsequent psychological evaluator, the child gave her reasons for not wanting to go on visits with her paternal grandparents:

> Then [child] told [second psychological evaluator] she is especially stressed that the [grandparents] might try to take her away from her mother. When asked why she might think that, [child] stated that they often threatened that she was going to live with them and never see her Mom again. . . . [Child] claimed she is "shocked" that the [grandparents] are her grandparents because they often insult her and her mother during her visits with them. . . . [Child] claimed that it is [grand-

mother] that insults us the most. [The psychological evaluator's statements cited by the trial court judge.]

Researchers have pointed to the role of the alienated parent in contributing to the negative stance that children take against them through that
parent's own actions. Johnston and Kelly's study found a range of factors
that could be concluded as contributing to a child's stance against one of
his/her parents. One of these factors was poor parenting skills on the part
of the parent whom a child refuses to visit (2004, 622-628) . Other actions
by the parent include threats to take the child from their resident parent
and the initiation of continuous court processes which leave a child
doubtful and insecure and only tend to reinforce a child's alignment with
the parent who is the target of the court processes.[5]

After many years of stress and uncertainty for the child in case US67,
the court found that the grandparents lacked the appropriate legal
grounds for bringing an action in their own right and that the case was
not properly a case of contested custody between two parents, because
the grandparents, who were carrying out the case in the name of the
father, were really representing themselves. The father in a statement
said he was not interested in custodial residence with the child, although
he supported the grandparents being granted residential custody of the
child.[6] The outcome of this case leaves open the possibility that if the
father had continued the court process, however nominally in his own
right, the outcome may have been less certain for the child. Whether
there would have been a transfer of residential custody to the father or a
never ending judicial process cannot be determined here.

In contrast with case US67, in which problems with visitation became
the foundation of using the child's opinion as evidence to be analyzed, in
Sweden the idea of the opinions of children being based on the right of
children to be heard, listening to the opinions of mature children is
viewed as arising out of the respect owed to a person. What impact the
opinions of older children will have on the process is less about analyzing
the meaning of children's opinions and court control over the actions of
children and more about the ability, due to maturity, of children to
understand the impact of having their opinions followed.[7] In case SW16,
which has also been discussed in chapter 3, the children, age thirteen and
ten years old, had grown oppositional to their time with their father. The
children were especially against the court ordered residential time of one
full week at father's house once a month. The nonresident parent who
was subject to the children's negative stance engaged in some of the
behavior described in Johnston and Kelly's research. The father was not
violent, but he said derogatory things about the children's mother. He
also made threats to "take the children away from their mother," a threat
similar to that made by the grandparents in case US67. He continuously
used court processes to enforce his visitation choices. The ongoing legal

process added to the insecurity of the children and increased their fear and negative stance toward the parent they viewed as taking them to court all the time, and so the children's attitude became increasingly negative toward him. The children in case SW16 made clear in the custody report their desire to continue living with their mother. The custody evaluator reported that, "Both children . . . without hesitation said that they want to continue to live with their mother." Additionally, "Both have said they are afraid of their father."

The problem of the children's refusal to visit with the father was attributed by the court to the mother for her inability to "hand over responsibility" of the children to the father during his visitation times. The court's understanding of this dynamic, however, did not devalue the children's voices. To the contrary, disregarding the children's wishes was viewed as more detrimental to the children than the assurance of a relationship with the estranged parent through transferring residential custody.

Case US45 was also a case in which the children were refusing to visit the nonresident parent. The case involved three different professionals and one psychological expert. The children, ages eleven, thirteen, and sixteen, through the attorney for the minor child, said they did not want to be made to visit with the father; however, the case focused on whether or not the mother was using the allegations of the oldest child tactically, rather than on the wishes and opinions of the children, and whether forcing visits would be harmful to them given the circumstances of the case. The oldest child had made allegations against the father for sexually inappropriate behavior. The allegations were considered credible. The oldest child's influence on the stance her other siblings were taking toward the father seemed almost as if her influence were viewed as more problematic than the father's inappropriate behavior. The expert assigned to carry out psychological evaluations and tests on the family, including evaluations of the two younger siblings, recommended joint custody and reunification therapy for all three children. In the clinical setting the children's opinions were analyzed and their own wishes used as evidence against following their wishes. The narrative of the events was given as if the family should have kept quiet about the issues the oldest child had with the father, and that keeping quiet about the father's behavior would have been the appropriate way for the older child to react to her experiences. The expert seemed to expect the older child to remain silent in order to preserve the father's standing with the other children. The GAL supported the recommendations of the psychological evaluator with the exception that the GAL did not recommend reunification therapy against the will of the oldest child. The court accepted the recommendations of the GAL, and the older child was not forced to attend reunification therapy; the two other children, however, despite being at ages where they could cogently express their preferences, were ordered to start a schedule of visitation with their father. The parent in this case had acted in a highly inappropriate way, which had caused all his children to lose trust in him. With the help of the court he was able to refocus the responsibility for the outcome of his own actions onto his children and to have his own voice and opinion heard over and above their wishes.

Case SW39 is a case notable for what it does not contain; namely, a prolonged investigation into why two mature children's cogent opinions should or should not be followed. As has been shown in the previous chapters, consistency in the familiar environment is a very strong component of Swedish custody recommendations; additionally, the criterion of "a relationship with both parents" is almost always viewed as in a child's best interest. In the case of older children, however, the children's wishes may have a greater influence on what form visitation takes and in some cases whether it takes place at all. Case SW39 involved two children aged fifteen and fourteen years old, who decided they wanted to live with their father instead of their mother. The children had lived with their mother since the divorce of the parents seven years earlier, but they had more recently claimed that the mother was not providing enough food or clothing and that alcohol was being used inappropriately in the maternal home. The mother denied the accusations of the children. There was no judgment made regarding the accuracy of the children's complaints regarding their mother's care. In addition to wanting to change residence and live with the father, the children insisted on not being made to have a set schedule of visitation with their mother. The evaluator noted that, "During the conversation with the children they have made clear that they want to continue living at father's house. The children have shown a maturity which shows that they understand the consequences of this desire and that they have thought through their wish." The custody evaluator also clarified that "The children want to decide when they will visit with their mother." There was no prolonged investigation of the children's wishes or review of the father's motives regarding the children's stance against a schedule of visitation. The court did not engage in trying to force the children into visiting. Instead, the court initiated an end to the process by respecting the children's wishes. The most prominent criterion was not ensuring a relationship with both parents, but rather allowing the mature children the freedom to calmly decide what their continuing relationship with their mother would be. It was left to the mother to restore the children's trust in her rather than attempting to use the law to restore the children's trust.

The *Cintron v. Long* case provides some evidence of what the outcome is for a child when a US court exerts power to force an unwilling older child into a relationship with a parent. US courts often regard and give greater weight to the opinions of mature children in contrast with younger children's opinions, however, this same maturity may result in a child

sharing the blame for the conflict; that is, a child in US cases can come to
be viewed as one of the individuals responsible for the conflict. In *Cintron
v. Long,* the trial court judge refused to let the child's potential for running away pressure him into accepting the child's wish not to visit with
the estranged father. The twelve-year-old child was estranged from her
father who never married or lived with the mother and child. The father
had only sporadic contact with the child throughout her life, including a
cessation of contact between the child's fourth and ninth birthdays. When
the child was nine the father visited a couple of times and then went
without contact for two more years. After this period of absence, the
father wished to reestablish contact with the child. The child was ada-
mant that she did not want to visit with him. The court was equally
determined that a child should not go against what the court had ordered. The appeals court noted the argument of the trial court judge in
reference to the issue of control, "He asked, 'Why is a twelve year old
controlling the issue of visitation?' He noted that 'while he was not going
to force the daughter into a relationship with her dad that is detrimental
to her best interest. . . . I've got to ask myself why is a twelve year old
controlling the issue of visitation. That's what my concern is.'"[8] The
vexed tone of the trial court judge implies the understanding of proper
child behavior as obedience to adults, "the do as you are told" idea of
adult/child relationships (James and James 2004, 3), and the implication
that whoever is responsible for ensuring the child is obedient has not
done a proper job raising her. Both of these characterizations of the child
were supported by the custody evaluator who was appalled by the
daughter's negative behavior toward the father and viewed the mother
as responsible for allowing the child to act in that way. Visitation was
unsuccessful, and the trial court judge felt that his authority was under-
mined by the child. The focus of the case was removed from the idea of
determining the best interest of the child, to that of characterizing the
child as a delinquent because she would not follow court orders. The
mother was viewed as negligent for her failure to force the child to not
only visit with the father, but to behave nicely when on the forced visits.
The father, on the other hand, was characterized as reasonable. He merely wanted to have contact with his daughter. Although he too was willing
to disregard her wishes. The court threatened to switch custody to the
father if the child continued to act improperly when on a visit. The threat
was carried out and custody was transferred to the father despite the
child's promise to run away. The appeals court eventually reversed the
trial court's decision, noting that before the court process started there
had been no areas of concern in the child's life:

> [T]here was no evidence that the child had adjustment problems in
> other areas of her life [before custody transfer]. In fact, until this litiga-
> tion the child participated in various athletic activities, dance classes,

cheerleading, and performed well, both academically and socially, in school. She was not in any trouble with authority figures and was not running away from home.[9]

Unfortunately, before the appeals court had the chance to reverse the trial court's decision, the child's stable past had been upended, and the child had spent time in both a psychiatric hospital and a boarding school. Erickson (2007) confirms the fact that other jurisdictions can provide similar stories of older children who, although lucid in their desires and reasons for those desires, are shut out from having any impact on the definition of what is in their own interest.

In contrast, case SW36 makes clear the impact of older children's wishes on the outcome in Swedish cases even when these desires go against the important Swedish criterion of continuity of environment, and even when such a change may reduce children's contact with one parent. In SW36 the parents had a long history of arguing over custody and contact. At different times in the post-breakup relationship the father had wanted a joint residence arrangement and the children had spent equal time at both parents' houses, but at other times the father was inconsistent in his contact with the children and they had lived mainly with the mother. Additionally, the father had a conflicted relationship with one of the children, whom he found difficult to control. The current dispute involved the mother's move with the children to a new area. At the time of the custody evaluation the children were living with the mother and visiting the father every other weekend. The father wanted either a return to the joint residence arrangement, or to be awarded residence of one of the children (split custody), but not the child he had difficulties with. Both children, however, made clear their wish to remain with their present resident parent and to no longer have shared residence. The evaluator reported that, "[Child] thinks that things are good how they are now. If he was to change anything it would be to see pappa more during holidays. . . . Pappa could come and visit them in their [town] sometimes." Although the Swedish court usually ruled in favor of maintaining the status quo in cases where joint residence was already in place, and similarly did not easily agree with a residential parent moving from the familiar environment, case SW36 was directed by the opinions of the mature children regarding their current situation and so the mother was given sole residence and the move was allowed.

REGARDING THE OPINIONS OF YOUNG CHILDREN

In the US, whether the opinions of young children are actively sought varies according to how the particular professional or expert views his or her role as a child's advocate, but whether children's opinions were sought or not, the influence of children's opinions on the definition of best interest was most dependent on the attitude of individual judges. US judges expressed the idea that young children should not be put in the position of "having to make the decision"; such a situation, in the court's view, creates a burden for children. The judge in case US18, for example, citing *Gennarini v. Gennarini,* emphasized the confusion that might arise when a child attempts to give an opinion regarding the adult event of a custody trial:

> A child caught up in the maelstrom of family strife may produce, to the psychologically untrained eye and ear, distorted and thus misleading images not only of the child's parents but of the child's own feelings; and those feelings themselves may be transient. [10]

In other words, rather than being viewed as a right of the child to voice an opinion, having an opinion can be viewed as a burden from which a young child should be protected, and if a child does voice an opinion this voice should be interpreted for its psychological meaning rather than as a true expression of the child's desires. With this in mind, very young children may not be engaged in conversation in any way regarding their opinions, and many of the US cases made no mention of the preferences of young children. Children were likely to be observed, however, either by the custody evaluator or the psychological examiner with each of the parents. This interaction was sometimes commented on in the custody reports. References were made by custody evaluators regarding whether the children seemed comfortable with each parent.

In contrast, when decisions are made about children in Sweden there is a greater imperative than in the US to set up situations in which young children can voice an opinion regarding the decision being made. For example, in case SW22 the report writer presented different scenarios of possible living arrangements to the children in order to engage them in conversation about the situation:

> We talk about the fact that when parents no longer live together the children can live in different ways. They can live more at one house than another, or they can live at both houses the same amount. We wonder how they would like it to be, and they answer that they would like to live at both parents the same amount. We repeat our question, and each of them answers the same way to the same question. First [the oldest child], says that she would like to have it as it was earlier when they lived at each house the same amount. Then we ask the [younger child] and she says she wants to live in both houses the same amount. During the whole meeting the children were watchful and cautious, but when we discussed how they wanted to see their parents, they were decided that they wanted to live equally with both. In a later meeting we discussed with them what was written in the report about what they said the last time. They were still definite that to live with both parents equally was their wish. [The social report writers' state-

ment in the custody evaluation regarding their interview with the children.]

In both countries, however, young children's opinions were easily put aside without much analysis of the children's opinion through reference to the children's age rather than to the content and reasonableness of children's wishes if the children's wishes did not support the view of the professionals, experts, or the judges. James, James and McNamee (2004, 189-202) have noted the impact that the age categories of childhood, tied to ideas of stages of growth outlined in theories of development, by theorists such as Piaget, have on the reception of children's opinions in a court context. Case SW8, for example, which was discussed briefly in chapter 4, depicts the way in which, although the opinions of young children were actively sought in Sweden, their wishes were played down when the opinions did not coincide with the social worker's conclusions regarding best interest. In case SW8 the child wished to live with his mother. There were pertinent reasons that made the opinion of the child in this case reasonable and understandable based on the history of the parent-child relationships. The parents had separated when the child was four and from that time he continued to live with the mother and his older brother and have visits with the father on a regular basis. Three years after the parents' separation, when the child was seven years old, the parents tried a shared residence arrangement. The mother claimed she entered this agreement under pressure to agree to a change in custody type by the father and custody evaluators. According to the child's schoolteachers the new arrangement was not working positively for the child (who had some special needs). The mother wanted to return to the sole residence custody arrangement with her as the residential parent. At the same time, she had accepted employment in a place too far away to make shared residence possible. The father was opposed to the mother's plan and the custody process was started. The shared residence arrangement had been in place for three months prior to the mother's new employment that required relocation. Despite the fact that the mother had been the primary caregiver and the child was used to living both with the mother and with his older brother, the father was given temporary sole residential custody. By the time the custody report was completed the child had been living in the new arrangement with the father for five months. According to one of the social workers, when interviews were being carried out at the father's house or with the father bringing the child to the interview the child expressed no preference as to his residential arrangements, even when asked how he would like things to be. But in interviews with the child when he was visiting his mother, he did express an opinion to the custody evaluator:

> [The child] spontaneously said during both home visits, without me
> raising any questions, that he wants to live with his mother. [The social
> report writer's statement in the custody evaluation.]

The first social report writer was not present when the child expressed
this opinion, but he was aware of it. The report writer did not make an
analysis of the positive or negative implications of following the child's
wishes. Instead, he referred to research that contends children eight years
of age or older do best with the parent of the same gender (Svedin 1989).
If children's opinions are to be construed as a human right, when children express opinions, their opinions demand a thorough discussion
when being weighed against any particular social science literature that
advocates universal prescriptions of children's needs. Universal prescriptions of children's needs are often in flux and in dispute, as in the case of
the thesis used by the social report writer, and so reference to social
science literature alone should not automatically outweigh a lucidly expressed opinion of a child.[11] The court decided that the father should
have sole residential custody. The court's reasoning for not giving the
child's preference any weight was that "the child would merely replace
missing one parent for missing the other parent" and "the child was not
old enough to understand consequences":

> Child is not old enough to understand all the consequences of his mov-
> ing to live with his mother. Child's opinion can therefore have no effect
> on the decision of who should have custody. [The court's statement in
> the custody order.]

The child's wish in case SW8 could not really be viewed as being *against*
his interests and so had to be discounted by connecting his mistaken
desire to his age; he was not mature, being only eight, and by his lack of
understanding of the consequences "he will miss his father in the same
way he misses his mother now." In this way the child's opinion could be
put aside, not in the straightforward sense that arises when a child's
opinion must be viewed as being distinctly against his own interests, as it
might be in the case of a child who wanted to live with a parent who had
obvious detrimental parental shortcomings. There may be discomfort involved for both the evaluators and the court in accepting the wishes of a
child of this age when a child expresses a preference to live with one
parent over the other.[12] In case SW8, however, there was no compelling
reason to go against the child's wishes out of concern for his welfare. In
other words, the child's wishes may not be what the report writer or the
court regarded as in the child's best interest, but neither could it be said
to be against the child's interest. The mother in the case was a fit parent.
Furthermore, until the recent past, she had been the child's primary caregiver. Importantly, his sibling (this sibling was not a child of the father),
who he had been raised with, also lived with the mother. For these reasons, it was understandable that the child might express a wish to contin-

ue living with his mother. Also, the child did indeed have experience of knowing what it was like not to live with his father, despite the court's pronouncement to the contrary, as this had been the actual situation for most of the child's life.

At least one US state, Nebraska, has tried to move away from a strict reliance on age and has incorporated a criterion that calls for drawing conclusions regarding a child's wishes based on the reasonableness of a child's opinion rather than on the chronological age of a child.[13] Even with such a criterion in place, however, a child's wish may not be enough to have a court hear a case for modification. In *Mara v. Mara*, for example, the trial court did not find a ten-year-old child's opinion as a sufficient change in circumstances that would grant a review of the original custody order.[14] Evidence pointed to the fact that the child's reasons for wishing to live with his mother supported that his reasons were not frivolous. The appeals court noted that, "He preferred to live with [mother] because he thought she provided an environment in which he could 'grow up better'; he felt as if he was treated better at her house."[15] The child's testimony was backed up by numerous witnesses, including two ex-wives of the father, who reported the rough treatment of the child. Witnesses from the school the child attended reported the custodial parent's lack of involvement in the child's education. The school counselor testified that:

> [Child] felt very lonely, unloved by his father . . . does not like [father's] current girlfriend or her daughter and is very afraid of [the father].[16]

The mother appealed the trial court ruling and the appeals court reversed the trial court decision. Although the child's opinion was noted in the appeal court decision it did not mention the child's opinion as a factor in reversing the trial court's decision.

In the US sample cases, young children's opinions were often not mentioned at all. If they were noted, children's opinions seemed to be used to reinforce the decisions of the court and the conclusions of the expert or professional:

> Finally, the court finds, based on the [mother's] testimony, that [child] would prefer to spend all five weekdays with her mother. Although [child] is still young, she is bright and articulate and capable of forming an intelligent preference. [The judge's statements in the trial court memorandum.] Case US5

The child in the case above was only seven years old. However, her wishes were in line with what the judge had already determined was in her best interest; that is, she should live with the mother and have a regular schedule of visiting with the father. The judge noted that other witnesses had testified to the child's unhappiness with her current living arrangement of shared residential custody. Also, the judge formed a negative impression of the father due to his taking the child hostage in order to extort a shared residence agreement out of the mother.

In case US41 the judge first stated that a child (six years old) was too young to form an intelligent preference:

> The child being but six years of age is not of sufficient age and capable of forming an intelligent preference in this case. [The judge's statement in the trial court memorandum.]

But the judge went on to use the child's statement to lend strength to the decision nonetheless:

> He has stated repeatedly that he wants to live with his Mommy and to go "home." [The judge's statement in the trial court memorandum.]

The father had kept the child after the summer visitation schedule when the child should have been returned to the mother. The judge found that returning the child to his primary caregiver was in the child's best interest.

In contrast, in case SW40 a five-year-old child was very vocal in his opinion; however, the process required that the child's opinion be discussed as if he was confused about what he wanted because the actions of his mother meant his opinion could not be considered. Although the mother had been the primary caregiver for the child and was still nursing a younger sibling, father was given temporary residential custody when the parents' relationship broke down. Mother had residential custody of the children's older siblings (who were not the children of the father in the case).

> [In a conversation with the social worker, the social worker explains to the child why they are talking.] That mamma and pappa are unsure where [he] and his brother should live. He [child] says, "I always think about my mother. It is far to go to my mother's house." [The social worker asked] How is it where you live now? [The child answered] "always at mamma's and perhaps at pappa's." We talk about where he will live and he says, "it is fun at pappa's but the most fun at mama's . . . maybe the same at each house. . . ." [Later he says] "when pappa says he will have a longer time than mamma I say no that is not fair they should have the same amount of time." [The social report writer's statement regarding the interview with the child from the custody evaluation]

Out of fear that she was about to lose residential custody of the children permanently, the mother abducted the children and took them to another country for several months. However, she returned and was jailed for the abduction and later given very restricted and supervised contact.

When the child was back living at his father's house another interview was carried out. The child told the social report writer, "Tell that judge guy I want to live with my mother." After the child made this statement the social worker decided not to have any more conversations alone with the child because she said "he was too involved in the conflict between the parents." It would have been more accurate for the evaluator to point to the fact that the legal implications of the mother's actions were going to take precedence over the consideration of the child's opinion, rather than that the child did not understand his own opinion which he stated very clearly. The case set up a very uneasy juxtaposition for the interviewer, between the requirement of considering a child's opinion as a right for the child and a case where the actions of a parent meant the child's opinion could take no part. Since the child was young this uncomfortable situation was resolved by connecting the child's age to confusion and not knowing his own mind, thus canceling out any further need to find out what the child thought about the situation.

The way in which laws governing the treatment of children are perceived in the two countries sets up a differing focus regarding the necessity to create opportunities for children to voice their opinions. In the US laws govern children for their protection. In Sweden laws provide children with recognition of their status as people to whom certain human rights are attached. In the US laws that govern custody proceedings include the consideration of a child's opinion as one factor that a judge can give weight to. Particularly mature children are accorded the ability to have their opinion considered in decisions made about them and so are offered opportunities to voice an opinion. Older children's opinions may not simply be regarded or disregarded, however. Instead, older children's opinions may be analyzed and the validity of their opinions put in doubt. Not regarding an older child's opinions out of respect for a person, but instead out of fear the child will take action can set up a situation in which defining the child's best interest is lost and instead the process becomes an exercise to control the child. The extent to which younger children's opinions are explicitly sought is more variable in the US than Sweden. US judges are wary of purposely setting up situations for young children to express an opinion, because US judges view such action as forcing children to take on the role of adults by having children "make the decision." Children should be protected from having to make a decision which is the responsibility of adults to make. In Sweden the right attributed to children to voice their opinion in decisions made about them can be viewed as status conferring. The right to be heard recognizes children as people to whom a set of rights should apply. In order to provide for this right, Swedish report writers tried to create situations in which even very young children could voice their thoughts and ideas regarding the situation they were caught up in. Despite setting up situations for young children to voice an opinion, children's opinions could still be set aside in reference to their age rather than through the weighing of the reasonableness of a child's opinion when the child's opinion was not in line with the conclusions of the report writers or the court.

Older children's opinions, however, were likely to be regarded and respected.

NOTES

1. The interests of the mother, who was abused by the father, conflicted with the wishes of the children, but the children's opinions received the greatest weight.

2. Swedish law has incorporated the provisions found in the UNCRC (Swedish Government 1997/98, 182). Although the US has signed the convention it has not yet ratified it. For a discussion regarding why there is opposition against the convention in the US, see, for example, Farris 2007.

3. All 50 states with the possible exception of Minnesota allow corporal punishment of children by their parents. Corporal punishment is still an allowable method of school discipline in 19 US states (Gershoff 2008, 20).

4. The grandparents were awarded visitation as was the father earlier in the history of the case. However, the father remained involved in the case in name only, and it was the grandparents who intended to have residence of the child if the father won custody.

5. Johnston and Kelly (2004, 622-628) noted "the common tendency of pre-adolescents and adolescent children to align with one parent against the other."

6. Additionally, the father lived in another state, which made regular visitation impossible.

7. Föräldrabalken 6 kapital §11.

8. *Cintron v. Long*, 2000 WL 943745 (July 5, 2000, Va. App.) (unreported).

9. *Cintron*, WL 943745.

10. *Gennarini v. Gennarini*, 2 Conn. App. 132, 137, 477 A.2d 674 (1984). In case US1, the judge noted that he refused to try and ascertain a preference regarding residence, on the part of the children, due to their ages, eight and six.

11. Van Houtte and Jacobs's (2004, 143 –163) research disputes the findings of Svedin.

12. Some children view shared residence as being fair and others have firm preferences to remain in one home. When distances between parents' houses are too great, however, shared residence may not be an option.

13. Neb. Rev. Stat. S 42-364(2) (Reissue 1998), which states: "The desires and wishes of the minor child, if of an age of comprehension regardless of chronological age, when such desires and wishes are based on sound reasoning."

14. *Mara v. Mara*, 2003 WL 1798935 (April 8, 2003, Neb. App.) (unpublished). Modification cases require a change in circumstances before the case is heard again to decide on a change of residence.

15. *Mara*, WL 1798935.

16. *Mara*, WL 1798935.

NINE

Conclusion

JUSTICE IN THE DECISION-MAKING PROCESS

It was shown that in the US continuity of care, linked with a primary caregiver, was viewed as a key factor in decision making in contested cases. The primary caregiver was most likely to be awarded residence with the children at the end of the trial if the primary caregiver was viewed as the caregiver the child was used to receiving care from, and if the primary caregiver parent was perceived as likely to cooperate in promoting the relationship with the nonresident parent. Since the primary caregiver was most often the mother, this focus resulted in more mothers than fathers ending the process with residential custody of their children. When the US judges declined to give residence to the primary caregiver, or transferred residence from the primary caregiver to the nonresident parent, the judge created a narrative characterizing the primary caregiver's psychological care as detrimental to the child. This detriment was seen to arise from the primary caregiver's inability to understand the necessity of the nonresident parent's relationship with his child. US decisions were refocused from trying to define a child's best interest to deciding whether or not a case should be viewed as a case of interference with visitation. A negative assessment of a parent's personality by the psychological expert could interact with the judge's character assessment in cases where there were disputes regarding contact between the child and the nonresident parent or where there were allegations of sexual abuse of the child. Since the nonresident parent was most often the father, cases focused on the need to keep or create a father-child relationship whenever there seemed to be a fear regarding the possible loss of this relationship. There was no assessment of what would happen to the primary caregiver's relationship with children whose custody or residence was transferred. Perhaps having assessed the primary caregiving parent in a negative way we can assume that a lesser idea of detriment was foreseen from the interference with this relationship by the new resident parent, or judges simply assumed the new resident parent would be more coopera- tive with visitation; as it turned out, this was not always the case.

In Sweden continuity of environment was a stronger factor than the consideration of a primary caregiver, but residence of children was un- likely to be transferred in order to ensure a nonresident parent–child relationship. Since the conflict was further removed from the break-up of the parents' relationship, many of the children's residence was with their mothers. This fact meant that most of the cases ended with mothers hav- ing residence with their children. Both parents, however, were viewed as having the same relationship to their children and with the same ability to carry out appropriate care for their children. The parent living in the familiar environment was likely to receive custody whether or not they had previously been the primary caregiver. When one parent represented both continuity of environment and continuity of care, however, a deci- sion to move a child from the familiar environment and primary caregiv- er to ensure the relationship with the nonresident parent was not consid- ered in a child's best interest. Removing a child from their familiar envi- ronment was only made in those cases where the parent's problem with alcoholism, mental health, or the wishes of a mature child weighed against keeping the child in the familiar environment.

KNOWLEDGE IN THE DECISION-MAKING PROCESS

A key difference between the US and the Swedish cases was the focus of the representatives of knowledge. In the US experts and professionals framed cases as ones in which individuals were the cause of the problem of lack of agreement on custody or visitation arrangements. This focus on individuals manifests itself in a concentration on the personalities of the actors in the process. It has been shown in this study that in the US cases there were different recommendations submitted by a range of profes- sionals and experts. This feature of the US process makes final decisions less predictable. The unpredictable aspect of the process feeds into a cul- ture that views conflict as a quest to prove one is right, because the prospect of being the party that is in the right is held out as a possibility until the end of the process. Additionally in the US cases, psychology was used to critique parents' personalities and to analyze the actions of indi- viduals according to this critique. There was a built-in gender bias in this approach. Mothers' actions were framed as signs of mental unhealth. Mothers whose actions were analyzed negatively in this way were viewed as a detrimental influence on the emotional health of their chil- dren. When mothers' behaviors were framed in this way, harsh judgments were made. For example, residence of children could be transferred to fathers and supervised visitation could be ordered. In contrast, the negative actions of fathers were viewed as bad behavior but within what was perceived as a normal range of male behavior. Regardless of gender, psychological testing tended to pathologize parents made to undergo psychological examinations; that is, the language of testing was used to describe parents in court orders and memorandums. The requirement for therapy for one or both parents and the children was part of the custody orders in 29 out of 67 US cases.[1] The requirement for therapy was in addition to psychological investigations that were carried out during the custody process. This feature of the US cases points to the fact that although professionals, experts and judges are seeking to define a set of actions and arrangements that represent a child's best interest, what they are doing is defining people.

In Sweden psychology is used as part of a method for uncovering information about the parents' relationship difficulties. Psychology formed part of the technique which used professional empathy in order to have all the participants in the process feel understood and to uncover the misunderstanding which was assumed to be the basis of the conflict, because Swedish professionals concentrated on what they viewed as a problem of relationships; however, they often left out of their frame the context within which difficulties arose. Imbalances of power, for example, and instances of aggression were framed as mutual inability to cooperate. At the same time, the Swedish professionals were able to analyze a wider range of possibilities for what the underlying problems might be when there arose problems in parent-child relationships than was the focus on personalities that so oriented the US cases. Additionally, in Sweden only one custody report resulted from the work of the social workers carrying out the custody evaluation. Only one recommendation was made. The Swedish court followed the recommendation of the custody report in the majority of cases. Thus, the most likely result of the court decision was known to parents before the final order was made. This fact, combined with the ideas regarding conflict as misunderstanding, led to last-minute agreements for custody and visitation arrangements between the parents in 20 cases. It has also been illustrated, however, that the parents often had a history of prior agreements that had broken down. In 15 out of these 20 cases, for example, the parents had come to previous agreements (sometimes more than once). The fact that so many of these cases previously had agreements that were unsuccessful points to the fact that the resolution of problems that led to the court processes were not being dealt with. In 7 out of these 20 cases, alcohol abuse or violence was an issue. Since the process focused on the relationship problems between the parents and minimized the contribution of these other problems there was always the possibility that parents would return to court when these problems again made custody arrangements unworkable. This feature of the Swedish cases points to the fact that although professionals and judges in Sweden are seeking to define a set of actions and arrangements that represent a child's best interest, what they are doing is concentrating on the relationship between the parents and the drive to have the parents agree on some type of arrangement.

THE PARENTS

In both the US and Sweden mothers tended to claim the role of primary carer. Fathers in the US did not dispute mothers' claims, but rather claimed they would be better carers regardless of who was the carer in the past. How the child was doing in the present custody arrangement impacted on the reception of this claim. In Sweden fathers pointed to the fact that children need fathers the same as they need mothers and the reception of this claim had more to do with continuity of environment and custody arrangement than one parent's claim that they would be the better residential parent. Problems arose in both the US and Sweden when protective parents wanted to have sole custody as a way of ensuring proper care for their children. Disagreements over medical treatment were more common in the US sample, whereas protective parents worrying about substance abuse was more of a problem in the Swedish sample. In both countries the protective parent needed to be careful not to appear to devalue their child's relationship with the other parent despite legitimate worries about care.

In both the US and Sweden violent conflict, verbal abuse and threatening was a common feature of pre-breakup and post-breakup relationships and often part of the parents' interaction at pick-ups and drop-offs. In Sweden the focus of the cases tended to frame the problem of lack of agreement on custody arrangements as a misunderstanding between the parents. Following this line of reasoning, if both parents are involved in a misunderstanding, no one person can be more at fault for the conflict. Instead both parents required equal understanding to help them resolve their misunderstanding. This focus meant that many of the crucial dynamics of the Swedish cases were not dealt with and may help to explain why many of the cases involved parents who had previously sought help to come to agreements or had been involved in prior court process to decide on custody arrangements.[2]

In the US cases understanding what courts view as violence and what they view as mutual aggression or bad behavior is crucial in understanding how the consideration of the issue of violence works in contested custody cases. In the discussions regarding policy, the fact of violence in contested cases is often discussed as if it can be put aside once there are statutes in place that have presumptions against custody for domestic violence perpetrators. The US sample cases show, however, that only some cases that contained violence were considered as if they might be cases that could fall under this criterion. The interpretation of the type and extent of violence that should be considered the type of violence which would activate this presumption varies between judges.

CHILDREN'S OPINIONS

It was shown that Swedish ideas regarding children's rights are tied to the idea of rights for children as encapsulated by the UNCRC and can be thought of as status conferring. This results in a situation congruent with the professional emphasis on empathy in Sweden in which even very young children should have a chance to describe their thoughts regarding the decision being made about them. In the US children are accorded a right to have their opinions weighed with the other evidence of a case. The criterion has different guidelines from state to state and so represents less of a universal guarantee for children. Due to the limited scope and variability of the factor, the criterion in the US can be viewed as action sorting. The right to have their opinions considered confers less status on children. Children's opinions may be used as evidence for making a decision in a case, but the opinions of young children may or may not be actively sought. For US judges the effort to try and have young children express an opinion is viewed as placing the burden of the adult decision on the child, or worse, making a child choose between parents. Even mature children, in the US cases, derived less status from the right to voice their opinions due to the fact that their opinions might be analyzed as psychological evidence rather than out of respectful consideration of their wishes. In both countries older children are more likely than young children to have their opinions followed. In the US, however, the impact of older children's opinions on the process is more variable and fluctuates between the idea that it is more difficult to control older children and the idea that older children need to be controlled. Control of children becomes an issue in contested cases, especially in reference to the criterion of having a relationship with both parents. When the wishes of children come up against the wishes of a parent, children can be viewed as the cause of conflict and, in the worst case, draconian measures can be taken to ensure children abide by court orders. In both Sweden and the US younger children are not viewed as capable of understanding the consequences of their wishes. The opinions of younger children, however, may be used to support the conclusions of professionals, experts, and the court when young children's wishes are in line with the conclusions of these individuals. When younger children's opinions are not in agreement with the conclusions of the court children's opinions are disregarded, mainly through a reference to the young age of the children involved.

OUTCOMES FOR CHILDREN?

The results of the cases have been depicted in terms of custody arrangements that were ordered. The result of a particular court process, however, in itself does not tell the whole story in the life of a child. For this reason a discussion of outcomes of these cases needs to be viewed as not identical with outcomes for children after a case has been decided. Particular attention needs to be paid to the fact, as a concentration on some of the longer-running cases illustrates, that in many cases the individual court processes are just a snapshot in a series of repeating legal confrontations between two parents. It is not possible to say if the particular court decisions, represented by the sample, were the end of the legal story in those cases or the end of the conflict between the parents. There is still less ability to say what the actual outcomes were for the children in the cases in terms of the impact on their quality of life and long-term emotional health. Contested cases can involve future court processes in addition to or besides an appeal of any of the decisions made regarding residence, custody and visitation. Future court processes, for example, might involve requests for modification of residence, changes in visitation arrangements, requests to move away from the common parental area, and contempt processes when problems with visitation or abuse arise. Drawing conclusions from outcomes of only one particular court action may miss this feature of court litigation which is bound to be crucial in the actual lived experience of children and therefore the outcome for children who are the focus of a case.

BEST INTEREST

If contested custody and visitation processes are studied from within one society, what is happening will always be described by judges, professionals, and experts as an attempt to define what is in the best interest of the child involved in the case; this definition of the process is circular, because whatever judges, professionals, and experts are doing will be defined by them as defining best interest. Viewed against an alternative set of actions, that is to say, from the outside, this definition of their actions and the underlying basis of the problem becomes less certain. The different orientations to defining what the problem is give rise to unique areas of concern in each society. In the US the focus on individuals renders supervised visitation being recommended or ordered for fit parents is a concern, and in Sweden the concentration on relationships and compromise leads to a concern over the lack of focus on violence and domination by one parent over another. Whatever society we live in, it is important that we recognize the influences that are at work when we construct our stories, especially when our stories will be what is thought of as what is best for a child, so that we can understand that our taken for granted acceptance of the correctness of our definitions might be misplaced.

NOTES

1. In 14 of these cases co-parenting therapy for the parents was ordered as a part of the final order.

2. Twenty of the 53 Swedish sample cases involved alcohol or drug related problems. Twelve additional cases that did not involve substance abuse involved violence in the relationship. There were only 21 Swedish cases in the study in which substance/ alcohol abuse or violence was not a significant component. Even within these 21 cases there were cases in which violence or alcohol misuse was mentioned.

Appendix

USING TEXT DOCUMENTS

Scott (1990, 20-35) outlines some of the issues that should be considered when using documents for research, namely authenticity, representativeness, credibility and meaning. The first step of analyzing the case material involved considering authenticity and representativeness. The authenticity of all the documentary evidence used in this study is reliable as there is a high probability that the documents are what they claim to be. Furthermore, analyses of the additional documentary materials, such as additional court materials, lend support to the overall conclusions of the study. The idea of representativeness, however, raises two concerns. First, whether or not the cases selected for the study are representative of cases of this sort. Second, are the documents studied representative of the population from which they have been taken? In a study such as the one undertaken here, it is also important to ask how much representativeness is necessary. For example, a small number of unique processes might illustrate points of comparison between the two case societies more effectively than a larger selection of documents considered to be highly representative. In other words, significant features of the process may be brought out through the comparison of cases which are not representative of contested cases as a whole (this approach is utilized in the analysis of cases in chapter 5). Leaving this assertion aside, the US and Swedish cases in this study are representative of contested custody cases in the US and Sweden when the factors present in the studied cases are compared with other studies of contested custody cases. These factors include the presence of violence and which spouse initiates the divorce in the US (Brinig and Allen 2000, 126-169; Jaffe and Geffner 1998, 371-396; Johnston et al. 2005, 284-94; Keilitz et al. 1997, 5; Kurz 1995, 158). Regarding the Swedish cases in the study, the economic characteristics of the parents and the presence of violence were in agreement with other studies of disputed cases (Rejmer 2003, 16; Eriksson 2003), and also the fact that contested cases do not represent a large proportion of the total number of parents seeking divorce in either jurisdiction. The numbers are around twenty percent in the US and ten percent in Sweden (Rejmer 2003, 16).

Representativeness in terms of population is a different aspect of the same issue. It is not possible to determine the ethnic characteristics of the participants in the US sample. References were sometimes made to the fact that a parent was from another country in the Swedish sample. If these references were not present it was not possible to determine the ethnicity of the parents and children. It is possible, however, to determine the economic status of both the US parents and the Swedish parents in the anonymously numbered documents. The US sample was mostly middle class, but variations do occur within this categorization, for example, lower, middle and upper middle class. This class distinction becomes problematic when an attempt is made to categorize mothers involved in US cases whose economic situation may depend mainly on their marital status. As the economic information makes clear, most of the mothers involved in the US cases were unemployed or employed part-time with low salaries at the time of the trial. The economic charts for both the US and Sweden outline the socioeconomic status of the parents in the anonymously coded documents.

TABLE 1

Case number	Mother	Father
US1	Blue collar	Retired
US2	Unemployed/homemaker	Over $100,000
US3	Below $20,000	Voluntary under-employed*
US4	Part-time below $10,000	Over $60,000
US5	Part-time/no information	Full-time/white collar
US6	Unemployed	$50,000 and assets
US7	No information	No information
US8	$50,000/white collar	Retired/wealthy
US9	No information	No information
US10	Part-time $25,000	Over $50,000 white collar
US11	Part-time blue collar	$200,000 white collar
US12	Unemployed	$50,000 white collar
US13	Part-time	Self-employed
US14	Employed blue collar	Army
US15	No information	No information
US16	No information	No information
US17	$25,000 blue collar	$72,000
US18	Employed	Blue collar
US19	Part-time/student	Blue collar
US20	Unemployed	$38,000 white collar
US21	On commission white collar	Unemployed (former higher earner)
US22	$14,000	$90,000
US23	$15,000	$30,000
US24	Unemployed	Blue collar
US25	Employed	White collar
US26	No information	No Information
US27	$23,000	$24,000 blue collar
US28	Unemployed	Wealthy business owner
US29	Part-time/training	Employed

*Voluntary underemployment is when one spouse chooses to be employed at a job that pays far below his or her historic marketable skills in order to avoid alimony or child support.

Case number	Mother	Father
US30	Employed	Unemployed
US31	On benefits	Business owner
US32	White collar	Retired/disability
US33	High earner	Retired
US34	Self-employed	Self-employed
US35	$60,000 white collar	$40,000 white collar
US36	Employed	Employed blue collar
US37	$14,000 blue collar	Disability
US38	No information	No information
US39	No information	No information
US40	Employed blue collar	No information
US41	Student	Employed blue collar
US42	No information	No information
US43	$18,000	$44,000
US44	No information	No information
US45	$60,000	$60,000
US46	Employed/white collar	Employed/blue collar
US47	Unemployed	$250,000
US48	No information	No information
US49	$13,000	White collar
US50	Unemployed (home-maker)	White collar
US51	$57,000	$21,000
US52	Unemployed (home-maker)	Wealthy
US53	$24,000	$74,000
US54	$21,000	$51,000
US55	$21,000	$220,000
US56	Employed	Employed
US57	Unemployed	White collar
US58	Unemployed	$55,000
US59	$36,000	$50,000
US60	Employed/white collar	Employed white collar
US61	Part-time $8,000	$58,000

Case number	Mother	Father
US62	Employed	Unemployed
US63	Wealthy	Wealthy
US64	No information	Wealthy
US65	Part-time $14,000	$49,000
US66	No information	No information
US67	No information	Employed/blue collar

Case number	Mother	Father
SW1	Employed/shop assistant	Early retirement
SW2	Unemployed	Unemployed
SW3	Employed/white collar	Employed/white collar
SW4	No Information	Employed/blue collar
SW5	Employed/ white collar	Employed/white collar
SW6	Part-time/blue collar	Sickness benefit
SW7	Employed/blue collar	Self-employed trade
SW8	Employed/white collar	Employed/blue collar
SW9	Employed/blue collar	Employed/blue collar
SW10	Unemployed	Employed/white collar
SW11	Unemployed	No information
SW12	Part-time/training	Early retired
SW13	Part-time/ blue collar	Training program
SW14	Employed/blue collar	Unemployed
SW15	Training	Employed/blue collar
SW16	Sickness benefit	Employed/white collar
SW17	No information	No information
SW18	No information	Sickness benefit
SW19	Part-time	No information
SW20	Unemployed	No information
SW21	No information	No information
SW22	Employed/blue collar	Employed/white collar
SW23	No information	No information
SW24	No information	No information
SW25	Employed/white collar	Self-employed
SW26	Employed/blue collar	Employed/blue collar
SW27	Unemployed	Employed/blue collar
SW28	Unemployed	Unemployed
SW29	Sickness benefit	Sickness benefit
SW30	Employed/blue collar	Unemployed
SW31	Employed/blue collar	Employed/blue collar

Case number	Mother	Father
SW32	No information	Employed/blue collar
SW33	No information	No information
SW34	No information	No information
SW35	Employed/white collar	Employed/white collar
SW36	Part-time/blue collar	Employed/white collar
SW37	Unemployed	Unemployed
SW38	Training	Employed
SW39	Training	Self-employed
SW40	Training	Employed
SW41	Employed/white collar	No information
SW42	Employed/maternity leave	Employed/white collar
SW43	Employed/white collar	Unemployed
SW44	Employed/blue collar	Unemployed
SW45	Maternity leave	Self-employed
SW46	No information	No information
SW47	Part-time	Training program
SW48	No information	Unemployed
SW49	Unemployed	Employed/blue collar
SW50	No information	Employed
SW51	No information	No information
SW52	Unemployed	Self-employed
SW53	Employed/blue collar	Employed/blue collar

The second step of the analysis of the documents involves Scott's issue of *credibility and meaning*. To what extent do the authors of the case texts believe what they have written or said? The sincerity of the judges, experts and professionals involved in creating the texts analyzed in this study has to be the starting point of the analysis. Although it can be imagined that other motives might hinder the construction of a court decision or a professional or expert recommendation besides an honest expression of how they view the details of a case, there is no evidence for drawing such a conclusion. The analysis of the texts, in this study, takes as its starting point the understanding that the judges, professionals and experts make both their recommendations and their decisions based on the sum of their knowledge and that what they have concluded through this synthesis they believe to be the best decision or recommendation that can be made in the particular case. As for the parents, their testimonies have to be interpreted while bearing in mind the possibility that they might not be truthful; a researcher cannot proceed without recognizing the fact that parents might fabricate stories or embellish arguments; however, when this judgment of lack of authenticity regarding the testimonies of the parents is made by a judge or the experts and professionals it also has to be critically analyzed.

Another consideration when looking at documentary material is that of meaning. This issue is part of the interpretive aspect of my study. For example, when reviewing the presence of violence in the cases, a stance to take relative to the meaning of violence had to be decided on. This problem of meaning in this instance was resolved by viewing violence as whatever judges viewed violence to be as opposed to considering violence as violence when mentioned by one of the participants. The latter approach was avoided due to the problem suggested above regarding the credibility of the parents. My approach illustrated the prevalence of violence in the contested cases being studied. Table 3 gives an overall view of the issues in each case and highlights the prevalence of violence in the parents' relationships. Within the context of this study, it has been found that judges have various interpretations of violence. For example, judges can view the mentioning of violence as fabrication or they can accept that it exists in a given case while at the same time seeing no clear instigator or aggressor. Alternatively, they can determine that one party acts as the aggressor but simultaneously uphold the view that the violence involved either does not impact on the case, or that it will not have any bearing on the decision. Finally, a judge might view violence as perpetrated by one participant and see it as a relevant factor in their decision.

Where numbers of cases in which violence is a factor are provided in this study, allegations of violence considered to be fabricated have been omitted from the totals. For cases in which the judge was unsure who was the aggressor a determination of who the aggressor was has not been made by the author. Leaving aside numbers for the moment, because this is a qualitative study, any discrepancies between a judge's conclusions in this area and a participant's experience have to be taken into account. This aspect can form an object of analysis without including particular cases in the totals of cases categorized as having violence in them. It can therefore be seen that where the meanings of particular categories established in this study come into play depends upon the focus of the analysis being made and that there exist different meanings for these categories depending upon which actors supply the meaning.

The text documents studied here, both those written by the judge as well as the custody evaluations are stories, the construction of which is meant to convince readers of the validity of the claims and conclusions contained within them. Each actor involved in the case either constructs their own version of events or becomes involved with the construction of one of the other actor's stories. It should also be clear that the legitimacy and power of some voices to shape and define the events of a case, as well as to define the other actors in the processes, is greater for some participants than it is for others. Particularly, a judge's construction of a story is what will become the truth of the events once a judge renders a decision. At other times, the custody evaluations made by the social workers or experts will be thought of as containing the truth behind the events.

ANALYZING DOCUMENTARY EVIDENCE IN TERMS OF THEMES

The texts produced from the contested custody process form stories with much in common with narratives found in books or news articles (both of which we also sometimes take at face value). Analyses of such material from a qualitative perspective involves deconstructing these stories in order to analyze which cultural factors operate within and influence the construction of the narrative. In other words, how did these stories develop? To both accomplish this, and also confound the taken for granted quality of these stories as they are presented requires the use of a method akin to throwing a deck of cards up into the air so that it is possible to see the parts of the process separated from the narrative. The method, however, also involves putting these parts back together in order to understand how the story might have been constructed; why has a particular story ended up in the form that it has? A template of questions was adopted for this method in order to try and determine which features in the documents were the most significant. Texts were broken down according to the questions below.

TABLE 2

Was the couple married? For how long? How many children did the couple have?
Was violence present during the together relationship or after? What form did any violence or abuse take? Who was considered responsible for it?
Who initiated the divorce? Who initiated the custody process?
Were there previous processes?
Who do the children want to live with? Does the process mention the children by name?
Do the children want to visit with the nonresident parent? Is there a new partner?
Does one parent want to move?
Is there a parent representing themselves in court?
What types of allegations are being made?
What type of custody or visitation arrangement do the parents want?
Are the parents finances disclosed? Are the parents employed? What is their level of education? What is their level of income? Do the parents have health problems?
Who were the experts? Who were the professionals? What witnesses were called?
Were there mental health issues involved?
Was there alcohol or other substance abuse?

In order to analyze the stories contained within the documents in relation to one another the material has been coded in terms of themes. This coding took place following a careful reading of all the sample documents involving the template above. At times the themes represent an occurrence, such as an instance of violence. At other times, a theme might represent the most prominent feature around which a story has been constructed by a particular actor, such as problems with visitation. Following a close reading of the 120 anonymous documents, it was noticed that certain themes were recurring. These recurring themes were violence and verbal abuse, substance abuse, issues of care and care-taking and trouble with visitation. Allegations of child sexual abuse were also included as a theme although this did not constitute a common occurrence in the cases; however, in the cases where this issue was present it was often the major organizing feature of the story of the case. Table 3 provides an overview of the features present in the anonymously coded cases. Table 3 also identifies the instigator of the process, the custody type ordered, and who it was ordered in favor of, and whether the decision was made in accordance with the opinion of the children involved in the case (wherever it is possible to determine). Table 3 also indicates whether the judge agreed with the professional or expert, and finally, if the decision reflected the preferred decision of the mother, father or neither (keeping in mind that whoever ends the process with residence is not always receiving their preferred decision).

TABLE 3

Case	Was sole custody awarded?	Who was the plaintiff? What did they ask for*?	Was joint legal-custody awarded?	Who was resident parent at the end of process?	Does the decision accord with the child's opinion?	Does the court agree with the professional?	Does the court agree with the expert?	Violence attributed to which parent?	Allegation of child sexual abuse made against which parent?	Alcohol Factor attributed to which parent?	Mental health factors attributed to which parent?	Who was awarded their Preferred Decision?
US1	No	Mother/sole	Yes	Mother	Unknown	Yes	In part	F	No	No	No	Father
US2	Mother	Mother/sole	No	Mother	No	No	No	No	No	Both	No	Neither
US3	Mother	Mother/sole or sole residence	No	Mother	Unknown	No	N/A	F	No	No	No	Mother
US4	No	Mother visitation issues	Yes	Mother	Unknown	N/A	N/A	No	No	No	No	Father more contact.
US5	Mother	Mother/sole or sole residence	No	Mother	Yes	In part	N/A	F	No	No	No	Mother
US6	Mother	Mother/sole	No	Mother	Unknown	Yes	In part	F	No	No	No	Mother
US7	Mother	Mother/sole	No	Mother	In part	N/A	N/A	No	No	No	No	Mother
US8	Mother	Mother/sole or sole residence	No	Mother	Unknown	No	No	No	Mother	No	No	Mother
US9	No	Mother/ relocate modify	Yes	Mother	No	No	Yes	No	No	No	No	Mother
US10	No	Mother/sole	Yes	Mother	Unknown	No	No	Both	No	No	No	Mother
US11	Father	Father/sole or sole residence	No	Father	Unknown	In part	N/A	No	Father	No	No	Father
US12	Father	Father/sole residence	No	Father	Unknown	Yes	In part	No	Father	No	Mother	Father
US13	Father	Father/sole modify	No	Father	No	Yes	Yes	No	No	No	No	Father

* In modification cases the plaintiff will be defined as the parent that started the current court action.

Case	Was sole custody awarded?	Who was the plaintiff? What did they ask for?	Was joint legal-custody awarded?	Who was resident parent at the end of process?	Does the decision accord with the child's opinion?	Does the court agree with the professional?	Does the court agree with the expert?	Violence attributed to which parent?	Allegation of child sexual abuse made against which parent?	Alcohol Factor attributed to which parent?	Mental health factors attributed to which parent?	Who was awarded their Preferred Decision?
US14	No	Father/sole residence modify	Yes	Father	Unknown	Yes/No*	N/A	No	No	No	No	Father
US15	Father	Father/sole modify	No	Father	No	Yes	N/A	No	Father	No	No	Father
US16	No	Mother/residence	Yes	Split	Yes	Unknown	Unknown	Both	No	No	No	Neither
US17	No	Mother/sole	Yes	Mother	Yes	Yes	Yes	Father	No	Father	No	Neither
US18	No	Mother/relocate modify	Yes	Both	Yes	Yes	Yes	No	No	No	No	Father
US19	No	Father/modify sole	Yes	Father	No	In part	N/A	No	No	No	No	Father/final decision-maker
US20	Father	Father/sole	No	Father	Unknown	In part	In part	No	No	Mother	Mother	Father
US21	Mother	Father/sole	No	Mother	Yes	Yes	No	Father	No	No	No	Mother
US22	No	Father/sole modify	Yes	Father	Yes	Yes	N/A	No	No	No	No	Father
US23	No	Mother/joint residence	Yes	Both	Yes	Yes	N/A	Mother	No	No	No	Mother
US24	No	Mother/visitation	Yes	Mother	No	No	N/A	No	No	No	No	Father

* **Judge agrees with the GAL but not with the Family Relations Counselor.**

Case	Was sole custody awarded?	Who was the plaintiff? What did they ask for?	Was joint legal-custody awarded?	Who was resident parent at the end of process?	Does the decision accord with the child's opinion?	Does the court agree with the professional?	Does the court agree with the expert?	Violence attributed to which parent?	Allegation of child sexual abuse made against which parent?	Alcohol Factor attributed to which parent?	Mental health factors attributed to which parent?	Who was awarded their Preferred Decision?
US25	No	Father/joint legal	Yes	Mother	Unknown	No/Yes*	Yes	Father	No	No	No	Father
US26	No	Father/visitation	No	Mother	N/A	N/A	N/A	Father	No	No	No	Father
US27	No	Father/sole	Yes	Mother	Unknown	In part	N/A	Father	No	No	No	Mother
US28	No	Mother/relocation	Yes	Both	Unknown	Yes	Yes	No	No	No	No	Father
US29	M/F	Father/sole and joint for other child	Split	Both	No	Yes	N/A	Mother	No	No	Mother	Father
US30	Mother	Mother/sole residence	No	Mother	No	No	N/A	Father	No	No	No	Mother
US31	M/F	Mother/sole	Split**	Split	No	No	No	No	No	No	No	Father
US32	No	Father/modify sole	Yes	Father	In Part	Yes	N/A	No	Father	No	No	Father
US33	No	Father/sole	Yes	Mother	Yes	Yes	No	No	No	Father	No	Mother yes/no***
US34	No	Mother/sole	Yes	Mother	Unknown	No	N/A	Father	No	Father	No	Father
US35	No	Mother/sole	Yes	Mother	Unknown	Yes	N/A	Father	No	Father	No	Father
US36	No	Mother/sole residence	Yes	Both	Unknown	Yes	N/A	No	No	Mother	No	Neither

* Judge agrees with the GAL but not with the Family Relations Counselor.
** Father received sole custody of two of the children and mother received sole custody of one.
*** Mother wanted to move away. Court gave mother residence if she did not move away.

Case	Was sole custody awarded?	Who was the plaintiff? What did they ask for?	Was joint legal-custody awarded?	Who was resident parent at the end of process?	Does the decision accord with the child's opinion?	Does the court agree with the professional?	Does the court agree with the expert?	Violence attributed to which parent?	Allegation of child sexual abuse made against which parent?	Alcohol Factor attributed to which parent?	Mental health factors attributed to which parent?	Who was awarded their Preferred Decision?
US37	Father	Mother/sole	No	Father	Unknown	N/A	In part	Mother	Father	Mother	Mother	Father
US38	No	Mother/sole	Yes	Mother	Unknown	Unknown	N/A	No	No	No	No	Mother
US39	No	Mother/modify residence	Yes	Mother	Yes	Yes	Yes	No	No	No	No	Mother
US40	No	Mother/modify residence	Yes	Mother	Yes	Yes	Yes	No	No	No	No	Mother
US41	Mother	Father/sole residence	No	Mother	Yes	Yes	N/A	No	No	No	No	Mother
US42	No	Father/sole residence	Yes	Mother	No	Yes	N/A	No	No	No	No	Mother
US43	No	Mother/sole residence	Yes	Father	Unknown	Yes	N/A	No	No	No	No	Father
US44	No	Father/modify residence	Yes	Mother	Yes/no*	No	N/A	No	No	No	No	Mother
US45	Mother	Mother/sole	No	Mother	Yes/no	Yes/no**	In part	No	Father	No	No	Neither
US46	Mother	Mother/sole	No	Mother	Unknown	Unknown	N/A	No	No	No	Father	Mother
US47	Mother	Mother/sole	No	Mother	Unknown	In part	In part	No	No	No	No	Mother
US48	Mother	Mother/modify to sole	No	Mother	Yes	Yes	N/A	No	No	No	No	Mother
US49	Mother	Mother/sole	No	Mother	Unknown	Yes	N/A	No	No	No	No	Mother

* Child keeps changing the parent he says he wants to live with.
** Court agrees with the GAL not with the Family Relations Counselor. The GAL's recommendations incorporate some of the expert recommendations.

Case	Was sole custody awarded?	Who was the plaintiff? What did they ask for?	Was joint legal-custody awarded?	Who was resident parent at the end of process?	Does the decision accord with the child's opinion?	Does the court agree with the professional?	Does the court agree with the expert?	Violence attributed to which parent?	Allegation of child sexual abuse made against which parent?	Alcohol Factor attributed to which parent?	Mental health factors attributed to which parent?	Who was awarded their Preferred Decision?
US50	No	Mother/sole	Yes	Mother	Unknown	No	N/A	No	No	No	No	Mother
US51	No	Mother/sole	Yes	Mother	unknown	Yes	N/A	Father	No	No	No	Mother
US52	No	Father/sole residence	Yes	Mother	Unknown	Unknown	N/A	No	No	No	No	Mother
US53	No	Mother/sole and to relocate	Yes	Mother	In part	Yes/No*	In part	Father	No	No	No	Mother/Father
US54	No	Father/against relocation	Yes	Mother	Unknown	Yes	N/A	Both	No	No	No	Mother
US55	No	Mother/sole residence	Yes	Both	In part	N/A	In part	No	No	No	No	Neither
US56	No	Mother/sole residence modify	Yes	Father	unknown	Yes	N/A	No	No	No	No	Father
US57	Mother	Mother/sole	No	Mother	unknown	In part	Yes	Both	No	No	No	Mother in part
US58	No	Father/sole	Yes	Mother	Unknown	Yes	Yes	Father	No	No	No	Mother
US59	Mother	Father/sole residence	No	Mother	Unknown	N/A	N/A	Father	No	No	No	Mother
US60	No	Mother/joint and more visitation	Yes	Father	Unknown	In part	In part	No	No	No	No	Neither
US61	No	Mother/sole	Yes	Mother	Unknown	unknown	N/A	Father	No	No	No	Unknown
US62	Mother	Mother/sole	No	Mother	Unknown	Yes	N/A	Father	No	No	No	Mother
US63	No	Mother/sole	Yes	Both	Yes	Yes/GAL	N/A	No	No	No	No	Father
US64	Mother	Mother/sole	No	Mother	Unknown	Yes	N/A	Father	No	No	No	Mother

* Court agrees with the Family Relations Counselor in part but not with the GAL.

Case	Was sole custody awarded?	Who was the plaintiff? What did they ask for?	Was joint legal-custody awarded?	Who was resident parent at the end of process?	Does the decision accord with the child's opinion?	Does the court agree with the professional?	Does the court agree with the expert?	Violence attributed to which parent?	Allegation of child sexual abuse made against which parent?	Alcohol Factor attributed to which parent?	Mental health factors attributed to which parent?	Who was awarded their Preferred Decision?
US65	Father	Father/sole	No	Father	Unknown	Yes	N0	No	No	No	Mother	Father
US66	Mother	Mother/sole	No	Mother	Unknown	No	No	Both	No	No	No	Mother
US67	Mother	Father/modify sole	No	Mother	Yes	In part	In part	Father	Father	Father	No	Mother

Case	Who was the Plaintiff? What did they ask for.	Was sole custody awarded?	Was joint legal-custody awarded?	Who was resident parent at the end of process?	Does the decision accord with the child's opinion?	Does the court agrees with the professional?	Does the court agree with the expert?	Violence Attributed to which parent?	Allegation of Child Sexual Abuse made against which parent?	Alcohol Factor attributed to which parent?	Mental Health Factor Attributed to which parent?	Who was awarded their Preferred Decision
SW1	Mother/ sole or sole residence.	Mother	No	Mother	Unknown	Yes	N/A	No	No	No	No	Mother
SW2	Father/sole custody	Mother*	Yes/No	Split	Unknown	Agreement**	N/A	Father	No	Father	Father	Both
SW3	Mother/sole or sole residence	No	Yes	Mother	Unknown	Agreement**	N/A	No	No	Father	No	Father
SW4	Mother/joint with sole residence	No	Yes	Father	Unknown	Yes	N/A	No	No	No	No	Neither
SW5	Mother/sole	No	Yes	Both	Unknown	No	N/A	No	No	No	No	Father
SW6	Mother/sole or sole residence	No	Yes	Both	Yes	Yes	N/A	Father	No	No	No	Father
SW7	Father sole or sole residence	Mother	No	Mother	Yes	Yes	N/A	Father	Father	Father	No	Mother
SW8	Mother/sole or sole residence	Father	No	Father	No	Yes	N/A	No	No	No	No	Father
SW9	Father/ sole custody	No	Yes	Father	Unknown	Yes	N/A	No	No	Mother	No	Mother
SW10	Father/ sole custody	Father	No	Father	Unknown	Yes	N/A	Father	No	Both***	No	Father
SW11	Father/sole custody	Father	No	Father	Yes	Yes	N/A	No	No	Mother	No	Father
SW12	Father/sole residence	No	Yes	Both	Unknown	No	N/A	No	No	No	No	Mother

* There was a split custody decision. Mother got sole custody of one child and father shared joint custody of the other children.
** Parents came to an agreement according to the recommendations of the report.
*** Mother had the greater problem.

Case	Who was the Plaintiff? What did they ask for.	Was sole custody awarded?	Was joint legal-custody awarded?	Who was resident parent at the end of process?	Does the decision accord with the child's opinion?	Does the court agrees with the professional?	Does the court agree with the expert?	Violence Attributed to which parent?	Allegation of Child Sexual Abuse made against which parent?	Alcohol Factor attributed to which parent?	Mental Health Factor Attributed to which parent?	Who was awarded their Preferred Decision
SW13	Father/sole custody	Mother	No	Mother	Unknown	Agreement*	N/A	No	No	No	No	Mother
SW14	Father/sole custody	Father	No	Father	Yes	Yes	N/A	No	No	Both**	No	Father
SW15	Father/joint custody/mother residence	No	Yes	Mother	Unknown	Yes	N/A	Father	No	No	No	Father
SW16	Father/sole custody	Mother	No	Mother	Yes	Yes	N/A	No	No	No	No	Mother
SW17	Mother/sole custody	Mother	No	Mother	Yes	Yes	N/A	Father	No	No	No	Mother
SW18	Father/sole custody	Mother	No	Mother	Yes	In part	N/A	Father	No	Father	No	Mother
SW19	Mother/ sole residence or joint residence	No	Yes	Mother	Unknown	Yes	N/A	No	No	No	No	Mother
SW20	Father/ sole custody and supervised visitation	Father	No	Father	Unknown	Yes	N/A	Mother	No	Mother	Mother	Father
SW21	Mother/sole or sole residence	No	Yes	Mother	No	Yes	N/A	No	No	Father	Father	Father
SW22	Mother/sole residence	No	Yes	Both	Yes	Agreement*	N/A	Both	No	No	No	Father
SW23	Father/sole custody	Father	No	Father	unknown	Yes	N/A	Mother	No	No	Mother	Father

* Parents came to an agreement according to the recommendations of the report.
** Mother had the greater problem.

Case	Who was the Plaintiff? What did they ask for.	Was sole custody awarded?	Was joint legal-custody awarded?	Who was resident parent at the end of process?	Does the decision accord with the child's opinion?	Does the court agrees with the professional?	Does the court agree with the expert?	Violence Attributed to which parent?	Allegation of Child Sexual Abuse made against which parent?	Alcohol Factor attributed to which parent?	Mental Health Factor Attributed to which parent?	Who was awarded their Preferred Decision
SW24	Father/joint custody	No	Yes	Both	Yes	Agreement*	N/A	Father	No	No	No	Father
SW25	Father/joint custody	Mother	No	Mother	unknown	Yes	N/A	Father	No	Father	No	Mother
SW26	Father/sole residence	No	Yes	Father	No	Yes	N/A	No	Father	No	No	Father
SW27	Mother/sole custody	Mother	No	Mother	Yes	Agreement*	N/A	No	No	No	No	Mother
SW28	Father wants contact	N/A	No	Other	unknown	Yes	N/A	Father	No	No	Mother	Mother
SW29	Mother/sole custody	Mother	No	Mother	unknown	Yes	N/A	Father	No	No	No	Mother
SW30	Mother/sole or sole residence	Mother	No	Mother	Yes	Agreement*	N/A	Father	No	Father	No	Mother
SW31	Mother/sole or sole residence	Mother	No	Mother	Unknown	Yes	N/A	Father	No	Father	No	Mother
SW32	Mother/sole or sole residence	No	Yes	Mother	unknown	Agreement*	N/A	No	No	No	No	Both
SW33	Mother/sole custody	No	Yes	Mother	No	Agreement	N/A	Father	No	Father	No	Father
SW34	Mother/sole or sole residence	No	Yes	Both	Yes	Agreement*	N/A	No	No	Father	No	Father
SW35	Mother/sole residence	No	Yes	Split	Yes	Agreement*	N/A	No	No	No	No	Father
SW36	Father/sole or sole residence	No	Yes	Mother	Yes	Agreement*	N/A	No	No	No	No	Mother

* Parents came to an agreement according to the recommendations of the report.

Case	Who was the Plaintiff? What did they ask for.	Was sole custody awarded?	Was joint legal custody awarded?	Who was resident parent at the end of process?	Does the decision accord with the child's opinion?	Does the court agrees with the professional?	Does the court agree with the expert?	Violence Attributed to which parent?	Allegation of Child Sexual Abuse made against which parent?	Alcohol Factor attributed to which parent?	Mental Health Factor Attributed to which parent?	Who was awarded their Preferred Decision
SW37	Mother/sole custody	No	Yes	Mother	Yes	Agreement*	N/A	No	No	No	No	Mother
SW38	Mother/sole residence	No	Yes	Mother	Unknown	Agreement*	N/A	Father	No	No	No	Mother
SW39	Father/sole custody	Father	No	Father	Yes	Yes	N/A	No	No	Mother	No	Father
SW40	Mother/sole residence or regular visitation	Father	No	Father	No	Yes	N/A	Father	No	No	No	Father
SW41	Father/sole custody	No	Yes	Mother	Yes	Agreement*	N/A	No	No	No	No	Mother
SW42	Father/sole custody	No	Yes	Split	Yes/No**	Agreement*	N/A	No	No	No	No	Neither
SW43	Mother/sole custody	Mother	No	Mother	Yes	Agreement*	N/A	Father	No	Father	No	Mother
SW44	Mother/sole custody	Mother	No	Mother	No	Agreement*	N/A	No	No	No	Father	Mother
SW45	Mother/sole custody	No	Yes	Mother	In part	No	N/A	Father***	No	No	No	Father
SW46	Father/sole or sole residence	Mother	No	Neither	Yes	Yes	N/A	Father	No	No	No	Mother
SW47	Father/sole or sole residence	No	Yes	Both	No	Yes	N/A	No	No	No	No	Mother
SW48	Mother/sole custody	Mother	No	Mother	unknown	Agreement*	N/A	No	No	Father	No	Mother

* Parents came to an agreement according to the recommendations of the custody report.
** One child changes her mind before the decision.
*** Father was violent toward the children.

Case	Who was the Plaintiff? What did they ask for.	Was sole custody awarded?	Was joint-legal custody awarded?	Who was resident parent at the end of process?	Does the decision accord with the child's opinion?	Does the court agrees with the professional?	Does the court agree with the expert?	Violence Attributed to which parent?	Allegation of Child Sexual Abuse made against which parent?	Alcohol Factor attributed to which parent?	Mental Health Factor Attributed to which parent?	Who was awarded their Preferred Decision
SW49	Father/sole custody	No	Yes	Father	Yes	Agreement*	N/A	No	No	Both****	Mother	Father
SW50	Mother/sole custody	Mother	No	Mother	Yes	Yes	N/A	No	No	No	No	Mother
SW51	Mother/sole custody	Mother	No	Mother	Yes	Yes	N/A	Father	No	Father	No	Mother
SW52	Father/sole custody	Mother	No	Mother	Unknown	Yes	N/A	No	No	No	No	Mother
SW53	Father/joint and shared residence	No	Yes	Mother	Unknown	Yes	N/A	Father	No	No	No	Neither

* Parents came to an agreement according to the recommendations of the custody report.
**** **Mother had the bigger problem.**

ORGANIZING THE PARTICIPANTS' COMMENTS INTO CATEGORIES

The third step of the method used in this study involved organizing the participants' comments into categories of conversations relative to the themes outlined above. The analysis of the cases considered love, justice and knowledge to be distinct sphere of knowledge claims represented by particular actors. The representatives of these discourses were analyzed in relation to the themes identified in the sample cases. For instance, how did the judges in the US cases view care, mental health issues and issues of behavior compared with the courts in Sweden? With this in mind, explanations of the actors were drawn out relevant to the themes for all the actors in the process whether or not they were the authors of the text. Mothers' and fathers' comments, to give an example, were linked to discussions of child care. All comments made by judges in relation to violence were also separated. Some themes were developed during this process, such as the amount of emphasis placed on a primary caregiver. The concepts of continuity of care and continuity of environment were also developed at this point. Finally, this stage in the process saw a development in how the documents outside of the initial sample should be considered. These documents comprise the extended court documents (appeals court cases) in the US case and the official documents in the Swedish case.

THE STATUS OF DIFFERENT DOCUMENTS

The types of documents that form the main focus of this study are texts created by judges including summing up, court orders, memorandums and appeals decisions. Evaluation reports are mainly created by social workers, but sometimes by lawyers. The evaluation report presents a recommendations based upon the area of expertise or professional knowledge of the evaluator involved. Additionally, the evaluation is meant to provide the judge with the background information of a case. In Sweden these evaluations are produced as if they contain the parents' accounts verbatim within the report. Conversely, US evaluations are presented as reports and do not include verbatim statements made by the actors; actors' statements are always noticeably paraphrased. This feature of the US evaluations makes it easier to see where the producer of such documents might tilt the evidence favorably or unfavorably toward one parent. In Swedish evaluations the extent to which evidence might be lopsided (more critical toward one parent than the other) was much less apparent. That is, in Swedish evaluations the parents and children are allowed to present their thoughts and feelings in a natural way. However, the extent to which it can be said that these are strictly verbatim accounts has to be viewed critically. We do not know what the social worker may have chosen to leave out, though parents involved in Swedish cases have a chance to review and comment on the evaluation. Evaluation documents, whether US or Swedish, do not have the same truth-creating status that the court summing up and the court order do. If the evaluator believes a particular event to have happened and the court does not, for the purposes of making a decision regarding the *best interests of the child*, the truth is framed in terms of what the court's understanding of the events of a case is. At the same time, the court depends upon the custody evaluations. The judges do not conduct out-of-court research regarding a particular case and so judges rely upon the evaluator's versions of events and the evaluator's descriptions of the individuals in any given case. The status of the evaluation document depends upon what other evidence is presented in a case, including whether the testimony of the parents seems to fit with the representation of them in the evaluation. Additionally, there are other materials available that a judge can rely upon in order to check the validity of an evaluation report. These include, for instance, court records that substantiate a history of domestic violence or arrest for drinking-related charges.

REPRESENTATION IN THE DOCUMENTS

For the purpose of analyzing the text, it is necessary that the elements of the text are separated from the representation of the elements. These elements include both people and aspects. For example, parents and violence. The form of all the texts studied, whatever their format, followed a logical and coherent order. The difficulty is looking beyond this coherent form and being able to see it as only one of a number of possible representations. If, for example, we take a statement in the text at face value, that is, without further analysis, then that statement might be viewed negatively, positively or simply as a matter of fact in reference to a participant. To put it differently, the air of truth of the statements made is imposed by the author of the text, shaped by the author's choice of inclusions and omissions. As Fairclough points out, dialogue involves turn taking. But in particular genres, such as report writing, the rules determining who is allowed to take their turn may be unequal.

> Dialogue in various institutional contexts often involves unequal restrictions on such conversational "rights." For instance, interview turns are likely to be assigned to an interviewee by the interviewer rather than taken by the interviewee, only interviewers have the right to ask questions while interviewees have the obligation to answer them, interviewers are more likely to interrupt interviewees than vice-versa, interviewers have greater control over topics and are more likely to offer

interpretations or summaries of what has been said, and to "repair"
what interviewees say. (2003, 79)

For these reasons, when undertaking analyses of texts, although the or-
ganizational and sense-making functions of narrative are compelling, the
researcher has to look to the foundation of the story and how it came to
be built up in the way it has. What social and culture features may have
oriented the creator's narrative? Also, the representations in the documents are not just representations of what went on in the legal process,
but are also representations of what happened in the relationship between the parents, and are sometimes representations or speculations of
what will happen to a child involved in the case in the future under
various scenarios that judges and evaluators create. These narratives or
representations of the actors and events can be positive or negative for
the individuals being described.

Finally, the analysis of the case material involved continually revisit-
ing the material to confirm or disconfirm impressions. Throughout the
process ideas began to develop through the comparison of the material
from the two case societies and these ideas were assisted by linking the
impressions to information derived from secondary material and extended primary sources.

THE CHILDREN IN THE SAMPLE CASES

In the US cases there were 28 cases involving one child. There were 27
cases involving two children and a further 9 that involved three children.
There were only 3 cases involving four children (US2, US16 and US17).
There were 121 children in the US sample cases combined. Thirteen children were in the 0-5 age range while the majority of children fell in the 6-
11 age range; 76 children to be exact. Thirty-two children were in the 12-
17 age range. Most of the Swedish cases were conflicts involving one
child (28 cases) or two children (21 cases). There was only one case involving four children (SW21) and the remaining 3 cases involved three
children (cases SW2, SW42 and SW50). There were 83 children in the
Swedish cases combined. Their ages ranged from 0 to 17 years. The most
common age for children in the Swedish cases was in the 6–11 age range,
which included 47 of the children. Seventeen of the Swedish sample case
children were in the 0-5 age range. Nineteen of the children from the
Swedish sample, were in the 12-17 age range.

PARENT RELATIONSHIPS COMPARED

The majority of the US cases involved couples that were once married; 59
out of 67 sample cases. In 7 of the 67 US sample cases the parents were

never married. There was only one example of a couple that never married and never lived together, case US13. Many of the Connecticut and Florida cases were happening in the context of a divorce, 48 of 67 cases. The exceptions were those cases which were to modify a preexisting custody order or where the parents were never married. The Swedish sample cases contained more nonmarried live-in relationships that had broken down (30 cases) than marital cases that had broken down (20 cases). A relationship in which children's parents are not married but live together is more common in Sweden than in the US. In general, however, there are more Swedish children who live together with their married parents than Swedish children who live together with their nonmarried parents (52 percent compared to 23 percent) (Statistiska centralbyrån 2003, 101-105). There were two cases where the parents never married and never lived together (SW9, SW23). Parents who have never married or lived together is a less common occurrence than cohabiting parents in Swedish society. For example, only 4.8 percent of children aged 16-17 years old in Sweden have never lived with both their parents (Statistiska centralbyrån 2003, 101-105). Swedish parents are granted automatic joint custody after divorce. In the case of nonmarried couples, if they had joint custody in the intact relationship then joint custody continued after the breakdown of the relationship. Only three Swedish sample cases, SW44, SW38, SW43, were in the context of the divorce of the parents; that is, where problems with custody and visitation occurred at the same time as the parents were going through a divorce. The Swedish court procedure separated issues of divorce and issues of custody. Overall, however, the Swedish sample contained a majority of cases where problems arose with the custody arrangement following a longer period of time after the separation of the parents (whether married or cohabiting) than did the US sample cases.

WHO INITIATES THE PROCESS, WHAT ORDERS ARE THEY ASKING THE COURT TO MAKE?

Swedish fathers who were the plaintiffs, or who might be thought of as the instigators of the process, were almost as likely to have asked for a sole residence arrangement as when a Swedish mother was the plaintiff. Swedish fathers were the plaintiff in 25 cases. In 15 out of 25 of these cases the father asked for sole legal custody. In 5 cases where a father was the plaintiff the father asked for sole residence and/or joint legal custody with sole residence. In one case (SW12) the father asked for sole residence. Swedish mothers were plaintiffs in 28 cases. In 12 out of these 28 cases the mother asked for sole legal custody. In 9 cases in which a Swedish mother was the plaintiff the mother asked for sole legal custody and / or sole residence. In 5 cases in which a mother was the plaintiff she asked for sole residence. Out of the 6 remaining cases the plaintiff father wanted joint legal custody in 3 cases (SW15, SW24, SW25). In one case the plaintiff father wanted contact (SW28) and in one case the plaintiff father wanted shared residence (SW53). In the remaining case the plaintiff mother wanted sole residence or shared residence (SW19).

It is difficult to determine which parent in the US cases could be said to have instigated the custody process, because most of the US cases were custody decisions in the context of a divorce case. In 43 of the 67 US sample cases the mother was designated as the plaintiff. In the remaining 24 cases the father was designated as the plaintiff in the original process. This characteristic of the US sample cases is in agreement with studies that show women in the US as more likely to initiate the divorce process (Brinig and Allen 2000, 126-169). At the same time, who was designated the plaintiff in a case document may not indicate who initiated the contested custody process. In case US46, for example, the mother started the divorce process and asked for particular orders; the father did not accept these orders and asked for his own preference for custody to be ordered. Mediation was not successful and a custody evaluation was ordered. In modification cases, where custody was either previously decided or agreed on by the parents, and provided for in the divorce judgment, the parent initiating the new trial may not have been the plaintiff in the original divorce case. The parent designated as the plaintiff in the new process will nonetheless be the parent who holds that title in the original divorce action, so that any inference regarding who is the instigator of the process cannot be made from that designation. There were 15 US cases post original custody decisions out of the 67 sample cases, and one case not in the context of the divorce of the parents (US26). When the parent who was the instigator is defined as the parent who brought a case to trial, including modification cases (whether or not they were the plaintiff in the original order), it was observed that mothers asked for sole custody/and or residence in 35 cases. In a further 8 cases mothers were the instigators asking for a variety of orders. When fathers were plaintiffs or the parent asking for modification they asked for sole custody and/or sole residence in 21 cases. In a further three cases the fathers wanted joint legal custody (US25), a schedule of visitation (US26), and in case US54 the father was against the relocation of the mother. The majority of the decisions in the US and Swedish sample cases involved a decision about where the child would live. There were 11 cases in the US and 11 cases in Sweden where the dispute did not involve the issue of residence but were conflicts about the type of custody (sole or joint) and visitation schedule the parents wanted. In most cases it was assumed that the parent not awarded residence would have a schedule of visitation, with the exception of cases SW28 and SW46, in which fathers were not allowed contact with the children.

WHAT ORDERS CAN THE JUDGES MAKE?

In both Sweden and the US, the dispute, from a legal perspective, is a matter of making a decision based on what orders the parents are asking the courts to make and what orders the courts are allowed to make. All the cases involved a decision regarding a particular custody type, residence arrangement or visitation schedule, or all three. Sweden, Connecticut and Florida can order forms of joint custody, joint legal custody and sole custody as well as setting out visitation schedules, who the child will live with or how much time a child will spend residing in each parent's house. In the US cases the judge might also order one parent to be the *main decision maker* on all issues, or the main decision maker on particular issues when the parents seem to be unable to carry out a joint custody or a shared parent agreement without returning to court. Sweden has no provisions for specifying an ultimate decision maker within a joint custody order. Recently, however, Swedish law has been changed to allow social workers to make decisions regarding whether a child should receive treatment over the objections of one of the parents in a joint custody arrangement when the other parent agrees to the treatment. Swedish courts can make an order of *gemensam vårdnad* (joint custody) or *ensam vårdnad* (sole custody). Florida courts can order shared parental responsibility encompassing the meaning of joint legal custody; that is, where the child lives with one parent but both share decision making, or where parents share parenting time as well as decision making equally. In the Florida sample, the court could make an order for residence in one parent's home (primary physical or residential responsibility). In Sweden joint custody orders could specify that the child live only in one parent's home and in whose home the child would live. The Swedish court could specify how much or what kind of contact (*umgängesrätt*) the nonresident parent and child would have with each other. In Connecticut and Sweden joint custody, legal or residential, could not be ordered if both parents were opposed to it. With the exception of this last limitation on the court's ability to make an order, the Connecticut and Florida court could make any orders regarding living and visiting arrangements for the child they found to be in the best interest of the child. Shared residence in the Swedish cases was not ordered where it was not already the existing arrangement. Swedish courts, however, may order shared residence to continue if it was the arrangement already in place at the time of the custody process.

In the US sample, changing a previous custody order is known as a modification case. A modification case means that the original custody order has to be modified in some way. This type of case involves a two-step method of decision making. A value is placed upon continuing living and visiting arrangements for children where those arrangements are part of a previous court order (these arrangements may be something the parents originally agreed on). For a modification case to be heard by the court, the parent bringing the case must prove a change in circumstances since the original order. Once this first step has been met the case will be decided based on the best interest of the child standard. This is an important factor to keep in mind, as those cases involving a transfer of residential custody within the context of an original order of residence for one of the parents have a double burden in overcoming the court preference for continuity and stability in arrangements for children. Before the first hurdle is overcome (a change in circumstance proven) a case to modify residence in the US is not simply a decision regarding which parent is the most suitable (or better) residential parent.

WHAT TERMINOLOGY DID THE COURT DOCUMENTS CONTAIN?

The US cases most often referred to the parties involved in the legal terminologies of plaintiff/defendant or petitioner/respondent. References to the father or mother in the US court documents did occur, but they were not the standard expressions used to denote the parents. References to "Dad" or "Mom" were uncommon in the documents and were used mainly in the context of speaking specifically about a particular child's relationship with his or her parents. The use of "Mother" or "Father" was more common, but here again mainly in a context directly related to the parent's relationship with the child or when talking about visitation schedules. In the Swedish cases the legal terminology *kärande/svarande* was used, which translates as plaintiff and defendant. In the Swedish sample the parents' first names were the means by which the parties were referred to both by the court and the custody evaluators. Joint custody in both the Swedish and US cases refers to shared decision making in the case of the child or children and not strictly speaking shared residence. In the Florida cases both contact and visitation were terms used by the court. In Connecticut access and visitation were used in the court summing up, but the custody evaluation might refer to contact as parenting time.

WHAT WERE THE LEGAL OUTCOMES IN THE SAMPLE CASES?

For an outcome to be viewed as in the favor of one parent over the other, it should be in line with what order the parent wanted the court to make. In the US cases it can be seen that in 29 of the 67 US cases the court awarded the father his preferred arrangement. This is not to say that the father was awarded sole or even residential custody, as the father's preferred arrangement was dependent on what the father requested. In 28 of the 67 US cases the mother was awarded her preferred arrangement. In a further seven cases neither parent was awarded their preferred arrangement and in the remaining three it was not possible to determine what orders the parents had requested. In 20 US cases the mother ended the process with sole custody. Residence in these cases may have been agreed on beforehand and only the custody type was in dispute. In 9 cases the father ended the process with sole custody. There were 7 US cases that ended with shared residence for the child. Thirty-one out of the 67 cases ended with the parents having joint legal custody.

Swedish mothers, in the sample cases, ended the process with sole custody in 19 cases and with sole residence in 10 cases. In 28 out of 53 cases the mothers ended the process with residence. In two cases mothers retained sole custody but the children did not live with either parent (SW28 and SW46). Swedish fathers were awarded sole custody in 8 cases. In another 5 Swedish cases the father was awarded sole residence. In 13 out of 53 Swedish cases the fathers ended the case with residence of the child/children. In 7 cases Swedish parents ended the process with joint residence. In 3 cases the parents had split custody where some children lived with one parent and other children lived with the other parent.

GENDER NEUTRALITY IN CUSTODY DECISIONS?

This study found that 8 of the orders for residence with fathers in the Swedish cases were due to the fact that the mothers in those cases had significant problems with alcohol abuse or other mental health problems. When both parents were suitable as residential parents for the child, however, the Swedish court was not more likely to change a current residential arrangement of the child if the father was the resident parent. The feature that could result in a change of residence between two equally suitable residential parents in the Swedish cases was the wishes of an older child. This leads to the conclusion that there is not a bias for mothers despite the fact that most cases end with the mothers having residence with the children. Instead, the greater number of mothers who end the process with residence of children results from the fact that in only a few cases were the fathers resident-parents consistently from the beginning of their children's lives. Furthermore, more fathers had substance abuse problems which added to the greater number of mothers given or retaining residence of the children at the end of the process. Mothers in the US cases ended the process with residential custody more often than US fathers. Many of the mothers in the sample cases were stay-at-home mothers or had significantly reduced their working hours to care for children and family during the marriage. Child care-taking is still a gendered occupation in the US despite the idea of gender equality stressed by the laws governing decisions involving children. In court, where continuity of care is often a factor in the decision making, although mothers and fathers are considered equally able to care for their children, mothers' actual past care tips the balance in their favor.

GENDER AND INTIMATE PARTNER VIOLENCE IN SWEDEN AND THE US

Studies of intimate partner violence between adults have depicted the gendered nature of intimate violence. For example, a Bureau of Justice report found that in 2001 women experienced 588,490 nonfatal violent offenses against them perpetrated by an intimate partner, while the rate for men was 103,220 (Rennison and Welchans 2001). An update of this report, and the most recent study on the issue from the Bureau of Justice, shows that in 2001 intimate partner violence primarily involved female victims (85 percent) (Rennison 2001). Other studies confirm the gendered nature of intimate partner violence in the US (Tjaden and Thoennes 2000). The National Institute of Justice (NIJ) survey found that women who were physically assaulted by an intimate partner were significantly more likely than their male counterparts to report their victimization to the police (26.7 percent and 13.5 percent, respectively). However the study reports that "...significantly more women than men chose not to report their physical assault to the police because they were afraid of their attacker, whereas significantly more men than women chose not to report their physical assault to the police because they considered it a minor or one-time incident." Tjaden and Thoennes concluded, "These findings underscore the fact that violence committed against women by intimates tends to be more threatening and severe than violence committed against men by intimates" (2000). Recently the plight of men abused by intimate partners has gained attention. Some researchers hypothesize that men abused by women are less likely to report such abuse to the police due to feelings of shame and emasculation. The findings of this study do not dispute that claim; however, such a dynamic did not come into play in these cases. Despite the ideal of gender equality in Sweden, Swedish society shares the gendered nature of intimate partner violence with US society (Eriksson and Pringle 2005, 1-12; Edin 2006, 10; Lundgren, Heimer, Westerstrand and Kalliokoski 2001).

Reference List

Amato, Paul R., and Sandra J. Rezac. 1994. "Contact with Nonresident Parents, Interparental Conflict, and Children's Behavior" *Journal of Family Issues* 15, no. 2 (June): 191-207.

Arendell, Terry. 1988. *Mothers and Divorce: Legal, Economic, and Social Dilemmas.* Berkeley: University of California Press.

Bala, Nicholas, and John Schuman. 2000. "Allegations of Sexual Abuse when Parents have Separated." *Canadian Family Law Quarterly* 17:191-241.

Barnombudsmannen. 2005. "Barnets bästa; barnombudsmannens synpunkter på fågor om vårdnad, boende och umgänge." In *Barnombudsmannen Rapporterar.* (br 2005:06) Swedish Children's Ombudsman.

—— 2005. "När tryggheten står på spel." *Barnombudsmannen Rapporterar* (br 2005:02) Swedish Children's Ombudsman.

Bateson, Gregory. 2000. *Steps to an Ecology of Mind.* Chicago: University of Chicago Press.

Benedek, E., and D. Schetky. 1984. "Allegations of Sexual Abuse in Child Custody Cases." Paper presented at The Annual Meeting of the American Academy of Psychiatry and the Law, Nassau, Bahamas.

Bogat, G. Anne, E. and DeJonghe, and A. A. Levendosky, et al. (2006). "Trauma Symptoms Among Infants Exposed to Intimate Partner Violence."*Child Abuse &Neglect* 30: 109-125.

Bowermaster, Janet M. 2002. "Legal Presumptions and the Role of Mental Health Professionals in Child Custody Proceedings." *Duquesne Law Review* (Winter): 265.

Borris, Edward B. 1998. "Parents' Ability and Willingness to Cooperate: "The Friendly Parent Doctrine" as a Most Important Factor in Recent Child Custody Cases." *Divorce Litigation* (10): 65, Part III.

Brown, Thea, Margarita Frederico, Lewsley Hewitt, and Rosemary Sheehan. 2000. "Revealing the Existence of Child Abuse in the Context of Marital Breakdown and Custody and Access Disputes." *Child Abuse &Neglect* 24 (6): 849-859.

Brinig, Margaret F., and Douglas W. Allen. 2000. "'These Boots Are Made For Walking': Why Most Divorce Filers Are Women." *American Law and Economics Review* 2 (1): 126-169.

Bruch, Carol. 2001. "Parental Alienation Syndrome and Parental Alienation." *Family Law Quarterly* 35 (3).

Bruner, Jerome. 1990. *Acts of Meaning.* Cambridge, Mass: Harvard University Press.

Busfield, Joan. 1996. *Men, Women and Madness: Understanding Gender and Mental Disorder.* Hampshire: Palgrave.

Campbell, Jacquelyn C., et al. "Assessing Risk Factors for Intimate Partner Homicide." *National Institute of Justice Journal* 250 (November): 14-19.

Casper, Lynne M., and Suzanne M. Bianchi. 2002. *Continuity and Change in the American Family.* Thousand Oaks, CA: Sage Publications.

Clark, Candace. 2005. "Theory of Sympathy." In *Sociology of Emotions*, ed. Johnathan Turner and Jan E. Stets, 56-63. Cambridge: Cambridge University Press.

Corsaro, William A. 1997. *The Sociology of Childhood.* Thousand Oaks, CA: Pine Forge Press.

Dalton, Clare, et al. 2006. "Navigating Custody and Visitation in Cases with Domestic Violence: A Judge's Guide." National Council of Juvenile and Family Court Judges.

Danforth, Gay and Bobbie L. Welling, eds. 1996. "Achieving Equal Justice for Women and Men in the California Courts." *California Gender Bias Final Report*, 121.

Daun, Åke. 1996. *The Swedish Mentality.* University Park: Penn State University Press.

Davis, Wendy N. 2001. "Some Lawyers Are Growing Hostile to the 'Friendly Parent' Idea in Custody Fights." *American Bar Association Journal* 87 (October): 26.

Dillman, David L. 2002. "The Paradox of Discretion and the Case of Elian Gonzalez." *Public Organization Review* 2 :165-185.

Dore, Margaret K. 2005. "The "Friendly Parent" Concept: A Flawed Factor for Child Custody." *Loyola Journal of Public Interest Law* 6: 41-56.

Ducote, Richard. 2002. "Guardians Ad Litem in Private Custody: The Case for Abolition." *Loyola Journal of Public Interest Law* (Spring).

Edin, Kerstin E. 2006. "Perspectives on Intimate Partner Violence, Focusing on Partner Violence on the Period of Pregnancy." Medical Dissertations: (number 04) Umeå University.

Edleson, Jeffrey L. 1999. "The Overlap Between Child Maltreatment and Woman Battering." *Violence against Women* 5, no. 2 (February): 134-154.

Elrod, Linda D. and Robert G. Spector. 2010. "Custody Criteria: chart 2." *Family Law Quarterly* 43, no. 4 (Winter): 972-973.

Erickson, Nancy S. 2007. Confusion on the Role of Law Guardians : The Matrimonial Commission's Report and the Need for Change. *New York Family Law Monthly* 8, no. 6 (February).

Eriksson, Maria. 2003. *I skuggan av pappa: familjerätten och hanteringen av fäders våld.* Sverige: Gondolin Förlags Ab.

Erickson, Maria, and M. Hester. 2001. "Violent Men as Good-Enough Fathers? A Look at England and Sweden." *Violence Against Women* 7:779-799.

Eriksson, Maria, and Keith Pringle. 2005. "Introduction: Nordic Issues and Dilemma." In *Tackling Men's Violence in Families, Nordic Issues and Dilemmas.* eds. Maria Eriksson, M. Hester, S. Keskinen, and K. Pringle. 1-12. Bristol: Policy Press.

Esping-Andersen, Gøsta. 1989. *The Three Worlds of Welfare Capitalism.* Cambridge: Polity Press.

Ewerlöf, Göran, and Tor Sverne. 1999. *Barnets bästa: Om föräldrar och samhällets ansvar.* Stockholm: Norstedts Juridik AB.

Fairclough, Norman. 2003. *Analysing Discourse: Textual Analysis for Social Research.* London: Routledge.

False-Allegations.com. http://www.false-allegations.com/html (accessed, June 21, 2008).

Farris, Michael 2007. "Advocates Prepare for the Children's Rights Treaty" *Parental Rights Organization Newsletter.*

Fergusson D. M., J. M. Boden, and L. J. Horwood 2006. "Examining the Intergenerational Transmission of Violence in a New Zealand Birth Cohort." *Child Abuse & Neglect*, 30 (1): 89-108.

Fields, Jason. 2002. "Children's Living Arrangements and Characteristics." *Current Population Reports*, P20-457 (March): 10.

Fineman, Martha L. 1988. "Dominant Discourse, Professional Language, and Legal Change in Child Custody Decision Making." *Harvard Law Review* 101, no. 4: 727-730.

Gardner, R. A. 1987. *The Parental Alienation Syndrome and the Differentiation Between Fabricates and Genuine Child Sex Abuse.* New Jersey: Creative Therapeutics.

Garrison, Marsha. 1996. "How Do Judges Decide Divorce Cases? An Empirical Analysis of Discretionary Decision-Making," *North Carolina Law Review* 74: 505-27.

Gershoff, E. T. 2008. Report on Physical Punishment in the United States: What Research Tells Us About Its Effects on Children. Columbus: OH: Center for Effective Discipline.

Ginzberg, Jeffery D. 1995. "Child Custody and Visitation: The Psychological Parent." In *Family Law Practice in Connecticut.* Chapter 10: Connecticut Law Library.

Goffman, Erving. 1986. *Frame Analysis.* New York: Harper and Row, reprint edition, Boston: Northeastern University Press.

Goldstein, Joseph, Anna Freud, and Albert J. Solnit. 1984. *Beyond the Best Interests of the Child*. New York: Free Press.

Gordon, Robert. 2008. *An Expert Look at Love, Intimacy and Personal Growth*. IAPT Press.

Graham-Bermann, S. A., and J. Seng. 2005. "Violence Exposure and Traumatic Stress Symptoms as Additional Predictors of Health Problems in High-Risk Children." *Journal of Pediatrics*. 146 (3): 309-10.

Green, Arthur H. 1986. "True and False Allegations of Sexual Abuse in Child Custody Disputes." *Journal of American Academy of Child Psychiatry* 25: 449.

Gunning, J. 1998. "Oocyte Donation: the Legislative Framework in Western Europe" *Human Reproduction*, 13: 98-102.

Hambya, Sherry, David Finkelhor, et al. 2010. "The Overlap of Witnessing Partner Violence with Child Maltreatment and Other Victimizations in a Nationally Representative Survey of Youth." *Child Abuse and Neglect* 34, no. 10 (October): 734–741.

Hester, Marianne. 2007. *Making an Impact: Children and Domestic Violence: A Reader*. London: Jessica Kingsley Publishers.

Holm, Ulla. 2001. *Empati: at Förstå Andra Människors Känslor*. Stockholm: Natur och Kultur.

Honneth, Axel. 1992. *The Struggle for Recognition: The Moral Grammar of Social Conflicts*. Cambridge: UK Polity Press.

Holt S., H. Buckley, and S.Whelan. 2008. "The Impact of Exposure to Domestic Violence on Children and Young People: a Review of the Literature." *Child Abuse & Neglect*, 32: 797–810.

Humphreys, Catherine. 1997. "Child Sexual Abuse Allegations in the Context of Divorce: Issues for Mothers." *British Journal of Social Work* 27: 529.

Jaffe, Peter, and Robert Geffner. 1998. "Child Custody Disputes and Domestic Violence: Critical issues for Mental Health, Social Service, and Legal Professionals." in *Children Exposed to Marital Violence: Theory, Research, and Applied Issues*. ed. George W. Holden et al. 371-396. Washington, DC: American Psychological Association.

James, Allison, and Adrian L. James. 2004. *Constructing Childhood: Theory, Policy and Social Practice*. Hampshire: Palgrave.

James, Adrian L., Allison James, and Sally McNamee. 2004. "Turn Down the Volume? —Not Hearing Children In Family Proceedings" *Child and Family Law Quarterly* 16 (June): 189-202.

Johnson-Weider, Michelle. 2003. "Guardian Ad Litem: A Solution Without Strength in Helping Protect Dependent Children." *Florida Bar Journal* 77, no. 4 (April): 87.

Johnston, Janet R. 1994 "High-Conflict Divorce," *The Future of Children*. 4, no. 1:165-182.

Johnson, Janet R., et al. 2005."Allegations and Substantiations of Abuse in Custody-Disputing Families" *Family Court Review* 43, no. 2 (April): 284-294.

Johnson, Janet R., and J.B. Kelly. 2004. "Rejoinder to Gardner's "Commentary on Kelly and Johnston's 'The Alienated Child: A Reformulation of Parental Alienation Syndrome.' *Family Court Review*. 42: 622-628.

Keilitz, Susan, et al. 1997. *Domestic Violence and Child Custody Disputes: A Resource Handbook for Judges and Court Managers*. The National Center for State Courts: State Justice Institute: Number R-202: 5.

Kelman, Steven. 1981. *Regulating America, Regulating Sweden: A Comparative Study of Occupational Safety and Health Policy* Cambridge, Mass: MIT Press

Kramer, Donald T. 1994. *Legal Rights Of Children*. 2nd edition. West Publishing Company.

Kurz, Demi. 1995. *For Richer For Poorer: Mothers Confront Divorce*. New York: Routledge.

Lakoff, George, and Mark Johnson. 2003. *Metaphors We Live By* . 2nd edition. Chicago: The University of Chicago Press.

Lampel, Anita K. 2003. "Child Alienation in Divorce: Assessing for Alienation and Access in Child Custody Cases: A Response to Lee and Olesen." *Family Court Review* 40, no. 2 (April): 232.

Landsorgnisationen. 2000. "Barnen och jämlikheten." *Rapport från välfärdsprojekt* [Swedish Trade Union Federation, children and equality].

Levin, Amy, and Linda G. Mills. 2003. "Fighting for Child Custody When Domestic Violence Is at Issue: Survey of State Laws" *Social Work* 48: 463-470

Lundgren, E., G. Heimer, J. Westerstrand, and A-M. Kalliokoski. 2001. "'Captured Queen', Men's Violence Against Women in 'Equal' Sweden." *A Prevalence Study*, Stockholm: Brottsoffermyndigheten. [Report online] http://www.brottsoffer myndigheten.se/.

Marie De Santis Women's Justice Center, Santa Rosa California. 2007. www.justicewomen.com/ help_family_law_4.html. Accessed November 21, 2007.

Mason, Mary Ann. 1994. *From Father's Property to Children's Rights: A History of Child Custody in the United States.* New York: Columbia University Press.

Mason, Mary, and Ann Quirk. 1997. "Are Mothers Losing Custody? Read My Lips: Trends in Judicial Decision Making in Custody Disputes—1920, 1960, 1990, 1995." *Family Law Quarterly* 31, no. 2 (Summer): 215-235.

Maume, D. J., and K. R. Mullin. 1993. "Men's participation in childcare and women's work attachment." *Social Problems* 40: 533-546.

Mechanic, David, and Stephen Hansell. 1989. "Divorce, Family Conflict, and Adolescents' Well-Being" *Journal of Health and Social Behavior* 30, no. 1: 105-116.

McIntosh, J. E. 2009. "Legislating for Shared Parenting: Exploring Some Underlying Assumptions." *Family Court Review* 47, no 3: 389–400.

Mertz, Elizabeth, and Kimberly A. Lonsway. 1998. "The Power of Denial: Individual and Cultural Constructions of Child Sexual Abuse." *North Western University Law Review* 92: 1415-1437.

Melli M. S., and P. R. Brown. 2008. "Exploring a New Family Form–The Shared Time Family " *International Journal of Law, Policy and the Family* 22: 231–269.

Ministry of Justice Fact Sheet. 1998. "Custody, Residence, and Contact." (July).

Mnookin, Robert H., and Eleanor Maccoby. 2002. "Facing the Dilemmas of Child Custody." *Virginia Journal of Social Policy and the Law* 10, no. 1 (Fall): 54 -88.

———. 1992. *Dividing the Child; Social and Legal Dilemmas of Custody.* Cambridge: Harvard University Press.

Moran, Judith D. 2003. "Judicial Independence in Family Courts: Beyond the Election-Appointment Dichotomy." *Family Law Quarterly* 37: 361.

Nissen, Morten. 1984. "Børn oplevelse af skilsmisse." *Danmark, Socialforskningsinstituttet,* (January).

Penfold, Susan. 1997. "Questionable Beliefs about Child Sexual Abuse Allegations during Custody Dispute." *Canadian Journal of Family Law* 14: 11-30.

Perry, Bruce D. 2005. *Maltreatment and the Developing Brain: How Early Childhood Experience Shapes Child and Culture.* London ON: Centre for Children & Families in the Justice System.

Philips, Susan U. 1998. *Ideology in the Language of Judges: How Judges Practice Law, Politics, and Courtroom Control.* Oxford: Oxford University Press

Pruett, Kyle. 2001. *Father Need: Why Father Care is as Essential as Mother Care for Your Child.* Re-print New York: Broadway, first printed by Free Press 2000.

Raitt, Fiona E., and M. Suzanne Zeedyk. 2004."Mothers On Trial: Discourses Of Cot Death And Münchhausen's Syndrome By Proxy." *Feminist Legal Studies* 12: 257–278.

Rejmer, Annika. 2003. *Vårdnadtvister,en Rättssociologisk Studie av Tingsrätts Funktion vid Handläggning av Vårdnadkonfliker med Utgångspunkt från Barnets Bästa.* Lund: Lund Studies in Sociology of Law.

Rennison, Callie Marie, and Sarah Welchans. 2000. "Intimate Partner Violence." *Bureau of Justice Statistics Special Report.* National Criminal Justice (May).

Rhoades, Helen. 2002. "The No Contact Mother, Reconstructions of Motherhood in the Era of the New Father." *International Journal of Law, Policy and the Family* 16: 71-94.

Roberts, Albert R. 2002. *Handbook of Domestic Violence Intervention Strategies: Policies, Programs and Legal Remedies.* New York: Oxford University Press.

Ross, Susan M. 1996. "Risk of Physical Abuse to Children of Spouse Abusing Parents." *Child Abuse & Neglect* 20, no. 7: 589-598.

Rumm, Peter D., and Peter Cummings, et al. 2000. "Identified Spouse Abuse as a Risk Factor for Child Abuse" *Child Abuse &Neglect*. 24, no. 11: 1375–1381.

Saldeen, Åke. 2002. "Family Law in Sweden" In *Family Law in Europe*. ed. Carolyn Hamilton and Kate Standley. 471-510. 2nd edition, London: Butterworth: 471-510.

Schiratzki, Johanna. 2002. "Barnrättens Grunder" Sweden: Studentlitterature.

Schmeeckle, Maria. 2007. "Gender Dynamics Stepfamilies: Adult Stepchildren's Views." *Journal of Marriage and Family* 69 no. 1: 174-189.

Schuman, Daniel C. 1986. "False Accusations of Physical and Sexual Abuse." *Bulletin American Academy Psychiatry Law* 14: 5-20.

Scott, John. 1990. *A Matter of Record: Documentary Sources in Social Research*. Cambridge: Polity Press.

Shuman, Daniel W. 2002. "The Role of Mental Health Experts in Custody Decisions: Science, Psychological Tests, and Clinical Judgment." *Family Law Quarterly* 36:135.

Singer, Anna. 2000. *Föräldraskap i rättslig belysining*. Stockholm: Iustus Förlag AB.

Sjösten, Mats. 1998. *Vårdnad, boende och umgänge*. Stockholm: Norstedts Juridik AB.

Stahl, Philip M. 1999. "Personality Traits of Parents and Developmental Needs of Children in High-Conflict Families" *Academy of Certified Family Law Specialists Newsletter* 3 (Winter): 8-16.

Statisiska Centralbyrån. 2004. *Barn och deras familjer*. Statisiska Centralbyrån: Sweden, http://www.scb.se.

Stoltz, Jo-Anne M., and Tara Ney. 2002. "Resistance to Visitation: Rethinking Parental and Child Alienation." *Family Court Review* 40, no. 2: 202.

Swedish Government. 1997/98. "Strategi för att förverkliga FN:s konventionbarnets rättigheter i Sverige." *Regeringens proposition*: 182.

Svedin, Carl Göran. 1989. "Vårdnad och umgänge." *Justitiedepartementets Promemoria* Ds1989: 53.

Svensson, Gert. 2003. "Ord mot ord om incestanklagelser." *Dagen Nyheter*, April 8, Insidan.   www.dn.se/DNet/jsp/polopoly.jsp?d=531&a=129192&previousRenderType=2.

Thoennes, Nancy, and Patricia G. Tjaden. 1990. "The Extent, Nature, and Validity of Sexual Abuse Allegations in Custody and Visitation Disputes." *Child Sexual Abuse & Neglect* 14 no. 2: 151-63.

―― 2000. "Extent Nature and Consequences of Intimate Partner Violence," *National Institute of Justice Research Report Findings from the National Violence Against Women Survey*. National Institute of Justice (July).

Van Houtte, Mieke, and An Jacobs. 2004. "Consequences of the Sex of the Custodial Parent on Three Indicators of Adolescent's Well-Being: Evidence from Belgian" *Journal of Divorce and Remarriage* 41, no 3: 143–163.

Wallace, Sara R., and Susan Silverberg Koerne. 2003. "Influence of Child and Family Factors on Judicial Decision in Contested Custody Cases." *Family Relations* 52, no. 2: 180-188.

Walsh, Michael R., and J. Michael Bone. 1997. "Parental Alienation Syndrome: An Age-old Custody Problem." *The Florida Bar Journal* (June): 93-96.

Warshak, Richard A. 2003. "Bringing Sense to Parental Alienation: A Look at the Disputes and Evidence." *Family Law Quarterly* 37 (Summer): 273-302.

Wickström. Anita. 2005. *Familjerätten: en introduktion*. Stockholm: Norstedts Juridik AB.

White, Hayden. 1973. *Metahistory, The Historical Imagination in Nineteenth-Century Europe*. Baltimore: Johns Hopkins University Press.

Whitfield, C. L., Anda R. F., S. R. Dube, and V. J. Felittle. 2003. "Violent Childhood Experiences and the Risk of Intimate Partner Violence in Adults: Assessment in a Large Health Maintenance Organization." *Journal of Interpersonal Violence* 18, no. 2: 166-185.

Whiteside, Mary F., Betsy Jane Becker, 2000. "Parental Factors and the Young Child's Postdivorce Adjustment: A Meta-Analysis with Implications for Parenting Arrangements." *Journal of Family Psychology*, 14, no. 1: 5-26.

Index

adversarial process, 19, 27n26
agreement, 62
alcohol abuse. *See also* substance and alcohol abuse
allegations, 7, 36; of child sexual abuse, 36–44, 44n9–45n11, 122, 133; of domestic violence, 33, 57, 58, 59, 75, 78, 101, 103, 104, 105, 107, 110, 114n2, 114n5, 148; false allegations, 18, 44n9–45n11, 104, 115n8; in Swedish cases, 42–44, 44n6, 150; of substance abuse, 93, 97
Allen, Douglas W., 141, 166
Amato, Paul R., 108
American Psychological Association (APA), 83n3
archetypal themes in literature, 13n2
Arendell, Terry, 23
arrest, 79
assumptions in contested custody documents, 7
Attorney for the Minor Child (AMC), 122; role of, 8, 9. *See also* professional
Azia v. Dilascia, 28n42

Bala, Nicholas, 44n10
Barnombudsmannen, 115n11, 117
Becker, Betsy Jane, 108
Benedek, Elissa P., 44n9
best interest of the child standard, 1, 10, 12, 17, 18, 21, 22, 25, 26; children's opinion's concerning, 117, 118, 119, 128, 129; historical development of, 2, 15, 16, 26n4, 67; in disputed custody cases, 34, 73, 76, 77, 79, 83n1, 88, 136; role of knowledge in defining, 47, 65n1; role of psychological assessment in US cases, 50–51, 60, 134
Bianchi, Suzanne M., 87

Boden, Joseph M., 113
Bogat, Anne G., 113
Bone, J.Michael, 70
Borris, Edward B., 32
Bowermaster, Janet M., 49, 65n1
Breitenfeldt v. Nickles-Breitenfeldt , 49, 65n3
Brining, Margaret F., 141, 166
Brown, Patricia R., 115n15
Brown, Thea, 44n10
Bruner, Jerome, 7
Buckly, Helen, 113

California Family Code, 26n3, 26n10
Campbell, Jacquelyn C., 109
Cappetta v. Cappetta, 44n1
care, 85, 86, 87, 88, 89, 133, 134, 136, 161; assessment of care in Sweden, 35, 61, 63, 64; care assessment in cases of abuse, 37; in cases of allegations of sexual abuse in US, 37, 38, 39, 42; character assessment and care, 29, 30, 33, 35, 133; concept of in Sweden, 3, 4, 25; gendered aspects of, 15, 16, 23, 168; and issues of alcohol and substance abuse, 93, 94, 96, 98, 136; and medical issues, 89, 90, 91, 92, 98n6, 99n8, 136; parental narratives concerning, 74, 78, 87, 89, 94, 103, 106, 108, 113, 130, 132n4, 133, 134, 138; psychological assessment, 32, 33, 56, 57, 60; recommendations based on gender Sweden, 61, 86; role of the social worker, 52, 63; violence in the parents' relationship, 105, 108, 109, 110, 111, 112, 113, 114, 136; when alienation is claimed, 69, 70, 79, 81
case characteristics, 151
Casper, Lynne M., 87